SUDDEN IMPACT

Leonard Renier

Wealth & Wisdom, Inc.
www.WealthAndWisdomInc.com

ISBN 0-7414-2964-0

Published by:

PUBLISHING.COM

1094 New DeHaven Street, Suite 100
West Conshohocken, PA 19428-2713
Info@buybooksontheweb.com
www.buybooksontheweb.com
Toll-free (877) BUY BOOK
Local Phone (610) 941-9999
Fax (610) 941-9959

Printed in the United States of America

Published November 2008

ACKNOWLEDGMENTS

There are people who have influenced my life and my way of thinking, who have helped me find the energy to write my opinions. My wife, Janice, whose love and support is the center of my life. She gave me encouragement to complete this task. My children—Jacqui, Colleen, Beth, and Zeb—who are with me every day in my heart and mind.

The people who expanded my knowledge in my business played an important role in my life. Don Blanton, founder of Money Trax, Inc., changed my career. His knowledge runs parallel with many of my thoughts. Much of my passion comes from the professionals across the country who I've been fortunate to meet. They are committed and dedicated, and are a tremendous source of knowledge.

At the office, Felicia Hull fights the daily battle of keeping things glued together and running well. Her support is sometimes my only sanctuary. Nothing can replace the nice things she, and all the other members of our office, has done for me.

CONTENTS

Who Should Read This

Knowing that certain events will take place in the near future, and knowing how they will impact your life, is information that you need in your financial world. Having this information is critical. Dramatic demographic changes in our country will place enormous demands on your financial future. How can you be aware of something that you're not aware of? Traditional thinking is not preparing you for these events that will change your life. For the average American, surviving financially will mean developing a new thought process.

I am working with a growing group of professionals from across the country who are deeply concerned about the direction we are headed as a country and the impact it will have on everyone's future. I believe that, given more knowledge and more information, you will be able to make better financial decisions. So, it is the goal of this book to create an awareness of the circumstances that will cause dramatic changes in your financial life. Having this awareness will help you prepare for a future that is filled with uncertainty.

Most people transfer away an enormous amount of their wealth unknowingly and unnecessarily. Wealth transfers, for many people, are caused by banks, the government, increasing taxation, credit card companies, finance and mortgage companies, and ever-growing personal debt. You are probably involved in the evolution of transferring much of your wealth away to those who create the situations, control the outcomes, and profit from it. Reducing or eliminating as many of these financial transfers, as you can, will change your life forever.

The dramatically changing demographics in our country and the transfers of your wealth are the two ingredients that will cause havoc in your financial future. The impact of these events will have lasting financial implications. Financial storms are forming on the horizon. Warnings have been posted. Prepare yourself: Change is coming.

Almost everyone can benefit from reading this book. If you identify with five of the following criteria, you could experience a defining moment in the way you think about money and your financial future.

- Strong household income
- Homeowner
- Married
- Family with children
- Participating in a retirement plan
- Educated
- Business owner, executive, or manager
- 30 years of age or older

This book is not about helping you pick stocks or mutual funds, or how to get "creative" with your tax returns. It is also not about off-shore banking, financial pyramid schemes, or creating red flags for the IRS. This book is about the future and how that future is going to change.

Intent

The intent of this book is to shed some light on the problems we will be facing in the future. We will break these problems down and analyze them carefully. Then, you will have a clear view of choices open to you. You will feel more confident and prepared to make better financial and life decisions.

And the Band Played On . . .

And the Band Played On. . .

In the still of the night, events are occurring that will change lives forever. A ship bound for the future leaving from the Port of Hope has struck an iceberg and is quietly taking on thousands of gallons of water per minute, yet everything is calm. In the ship's bridge, the captain nervously fingers through the ship's manual, searching for a solution that doesn't exist. Even though there is imminent danger, the order is given to the crew: "Remain calm, straighten the decks, smile, and tip your cap to the passengers." On the top deck, passengers, unaware of current events, listen passively as the band plays on. The band performs all the same tunes from the past, masking the up-and-coming moments of urgency and peril. Meanwhile, fifty feet below, structural flaws in the ship only compound the problem. Designers of the ship never expected this type of crisis, and the band plays on.

The captain now faces another decision. Should he prepare the passengers for the coming event, or hold out for the hope of a rescue? His training, experience, and pride have never exposed him to this type of problem. His choices are limited, as is his knowledge of such a crisis. He chooses to delay his decision, and orders the band to play on.

After an hour, it starts to become apparent even to the passengers that something is not right. Even though they are being told that everything is normal, there is uneasiness. A woman notices that the wine in her glass leans to one side. A man realizes that the ship has slowed to a snail's pace. Passengers begin to mumble amongst themselves about events that surround them, yet the band plays on.

The eerie part is that you and I are on the deck of this ship. We are caught playing a dangerous game, casually believing none of these events will affect us. Yet no one can deny, from the designers of the ship to the captain and the crew, that we have all entered into a dangerous time. A crisis is developing that will impact everyone, but no one seems to care, and the band plays on.

Victims of the Iceberg

As I stand next to you on the deck of this ship, it is the common thought of the common man to believe that all of this is the fault of the iceberg. It will be believed that the sudden impact of the ship and the iceberg caused this terrible fate. When, in all reality, 90% of all the problems on this night were created long before these two large objects touched. From the design of the ship, to the course that was charted, to the training of the crew, to the leadership of the captain, the iceberg only accelerated the problems that were already there. No one had prepared for this event. NO ONE. We are all destined for the same fate if we don't prepare differently. If you don't want to prepare, then simply lean back and enjoy the music, as the band plays on.

You Can't Be Aware of Something You're Not Aware Of

Many of us share the fate of the captain of the ship. Had he been made aware that icebergs existed in the area of the ship, he would have prepared differently. If he had the knowledge and information beforehand, the outcome could have been avoided. Without this information, the choices and options of the captain were limited. As a result, we are all left standing at the ship's railing watching the water rise with only one option, and it's not a very good one. Man the lifeboats, if there are any. Circumstances have forced us into this decision under duress.

Many of life's decisions are resolved in the same manner. There are a limited number of solutions simply because we are not aware of any others. When your options and knowledge are limited, outcomes are predictable, and the band plays on.

Survivability

If you could predict accurately what was

going to happen in your life in the next 3,000 days, would having that information help you make better decisions? I'm not talking about guessing football scores. I'm talking about using common sense and knowledge to help you come to the conclusion that certain events could, will, and are going to happen. You don't have to be a genius to figure this out.

If you earned $50,000 a year but every year you spent $55,000, it would be fairly easy to figure out that you will be in debt and heading for financial trouble. According to *The Daily Reckoning*, last year the United States had recorded an overall credit expansion of $2,718.6 billion while there was virtually no increase in national savings.[1] From a common-sense approach, one might begin to believe that the relationship between debt and decreasing savings will be a major problem for everyone in the near future. Alan Greenspan once asked a question, "How do we know when irrational exuberance has unduly escalated asset values which then become subject to unexpected and prolonged contractions?"[2] Currently, Americans are holding on to about $50 trillion in debt. This amount of debt is more than three times the total number of dollars in existence anywhere. As a country, we have hit an iceberg, we're taking on water, and the band plays on, as if nothing has happened.

---

[1] http://www.dailyreckoning.com.
[2] Remarks by Alan Greenspan, *Saving for Retirement*, at the 2002 National Summit of Retirement Savings, Department of Labor, Washington, D.C., February 28, 2002.

It's Time to Get Serious

Your economic situation is a matter of choice, not a matter of chance. Misguided and self-inflicted, it is centered on the lack of knowledge. Driven by fear, and cautious of change, financial decisions are made by default, without knowledge and unaware of unintended consequences.

Today, the vast majority of people are troubled and confused about the economy. They have been bombarded by the media, bullied by salespeople, and bewildered by the millions of things they feel they need to know. Over the past several years, they have seen all the financial lessons they learned in the 1980s and 1990s, and even recently, fail them. They know they can't live on four and five percent rates of return, yet they are scared and hesitant to make crucial decisions necessary to survive in today's economy. To make matters worse, right now, 90 million Americans are faced with the most critical investment challenges of their lives.[3]

We are going to shed some light on this darkness. We will break this problem down and analyze it carefully. Then, you will have a clear view of choices open to you. You will feel more confident and prepared to make financial decisions.

If something you thought to be true wasn't true, when would you want to know about it? That

---

[3] Maselli, Frank. *Seminars The Emotional Dynamic*. PowerSpeak, Inc., Franklin, Massachusetts, 1996.

defining moment in your financial world comes with the understanding of the efficiency of money. It is a simple yet effective method of uncovering and reducing transfers of your wealth that occur every day, unknowingly and unnecessarily. Learning to recapture these transfers in your financial life will change your life forever.

Fear or Knowledge

In order to understand the efficiency of money, we really have to study where we received our financial knowledge in the first place. Much of this knowledge came from our parents, who obtained wisdom from their parents. The factors which brought them to their financial decisions were totally different than the factors we are dealing with today. Most of their decisions were based on fear, not knowledge, and fear is the most prevalent lesson they passed to us. Financial decisions that are driven by fear are emotional decisions, and have very little to do with the facts.

Fortunately, over the last 50 years, financially, things have changed. The country has become a greater power, and, personally, we have created lifestyles that are the envy of the world. Unfortunately, in those 50 years, personal financial concepts and ideas have not changed with the times. The old financial lessons are being swallowed by the new world economy and a lack of personal financial responsibility.

All too often, we are told <u>what</u> to think, not <u>how</u> to think. Whether it is true or not, if you hear something repetitively, and it is told to you by enough people, you may perceive it to be true. Six thousand months ago, it was scientifically believed that the world, our planet, was flat. About 600 months ago, it was believed that no one could run a mile in less than four minutes. It was believed that anyone trying to disprove these notions would meet certain death. It wasn't until sailors sailed off into the sunset and disappeared from sight (falling off the edge of the earth) that a whole new world was discovered. It wasn't until Roger Banister ran a sub-four minute mile in the 1950s and lived to talk about it that these thought processes were proven wrong. Now, every week, someone is running a sub-four minute mile, and every day, people sail off into the sunset to discover new places and ideas.

Opinions and Facts

Many of our financial decisions are based on opinions that are not necessarily grounded in fact. To give you an example, the next time you're at a hospital, go up to the maternity ward and look at the newborns. There may be a baby there that, in a cute way, is sort of ugly. You would never be able to convince the mother of that baby that her baby is ugly. In the financial world, there may be some ideas that are truly ugly, but trying to convince that person that their ideas are ugly, even using proven financial facts, will be impossible. Many times, human nature will not allow us to change because we would have to admit that we were wrong and that our financial baby truly is ugly.

Understanding that what we are told to believe may not necessarily be true, and that our opinions can be stronger than facts, we can start the process of changing the way we think. Once again, all too often, we are told <u>what</u> to think. In this process, you will discover how to recognize what beliefs are opinions, and which ones are facts. You will discover the difference between myth and reality.

Remember, if something you thought to be true wasn't true, when would you want to know about it? Now or later? Almost all the decisions we make in life are based on our emotions, not necessarily on facts . . . why? Because we lack the knowledge and confidence to make really good decisions. If you had more knowledge, making decisions would be easier. Decisions should be made on the basis of facts, rather than emotions and/or fear. First, you must realize the problem, analyze it carefully, and have enough knowledge to create solutions. But most of all, you must have the courage to change.

Perception:
What You Really See and Know

To demonstrate perception, walk into your kitchen and look around. Now, just for fun, stand on a chair or on your kitchen table and look around the same room. All of a sudden, you see that room from a different perspective. You notice things you never noticed before, even though nothing has changed and you have been in that room thousands of times before.

Being able to see something from a different perspective will create different thoughts and ideas about what you see and what you didn't see. Congratulations, you may have discovered something that was right before your eyes, but didn't know how to discover it. With a different perspective, you can.

Traditionally, we have been taught that there is only one way to make money grow: To get a higher rate of return on the money. But, who is the one at risk in this quest? You, or the one making the recommendation? There is another way to make your money grow, but it is often overlooked. It is called the Efficiency of Money. To get a better understanding of this, you must think on a different level to get a clearer view of what is happening in your financial world.

First, you must understand that there are only

three types of money in your life . . . lifestyle, accumulated, and transferred money. Your lifestyle money is the money you spend to maintain your standard of living. Accumulated money is the money you try to save, and transferred money is the money that you spend and give away, sometimes unknowingly and unnecessarily. It is in transferred money where you lose most of your wealth. Unfortunately, this is where your perceptions become greater than your knowledge.

You have probably been approached by financial people, and their approach to you may sound something like this . . . "How much money do you have? Where is it invested? Oh, we can do better than that." How much time do you really want to spend reducing your lifestyle, so you could save more money? NOT MUCH! But if you were able to recapture some of the money that you were unknowingly and unnecessarily transferring away to others and save that money, do you feel that is the type of planning you would like to pursue? To give you an example, take a look at a family earning $75,000 per year. They are saving $5,000 per year, and they feel they are doing a great job. After their savings, what remains is $70,000 of residual income. That money is spent on food, housing, clothing, and taxes, and basically makes up their standard of living. At the end of the year, more times than not, this money has been spent and transferred away. There is nothing left. If they could save just 1% of that $70,000 they are transferring away, it would equal a 14% increase in their savings. (1% of $70,000 = $700 = 14% increase on $5,000). As you can see, learning to recapture these transfers would be a great benefit to everyone.

There are many forms of transfers, but the largest by far is taxes. The average household hands out about 50% of its earned wealth for direct and indirect taxes. For whose benefit do we labor, ours, the banks', or the government's? Financial advice given by the government and the banks has created record profits for banks and record tax revenues collected by the government. Here are the Ten Major Transfers that may be part of your life:

<u>10 Major Transfers</u>
Taxes
Tax Refunds
Qualified Retirement Programs
Owning a Home
Credit Cards
Financial Planning
Investments
Purchasing Cars
Life Insurance
Disability

It is no longer enough to simply invest money without understanding the unintended consequences that will confront you financially in the future. Understanding the changes that are going to occur in the near future could dramatically alter any financial planning that you may have considered.

Today, we have uncovered some of the problems that we will have to confront in the near future. They could change your personal finances tremendously. Given this information now could help you eliminate or reduce future financial trauma. This is not about the financial products you own—rather what you know about controlling your money. Without this knowledge, you will simply become the perfect taxpayer.

The Demon in Demographics

In 3,000 days, about 60 percent of the now-working population will be 55 years old or older. This is a certainty! Unfortunately, this leaves one-third of the now-working population to pay for all the government social programs for a majority of retired citizens. To compound the problem, the costs of social programs such as Medicaid, Medicare, and Social Security increase every year. This leaves little doubt that increased taxation will be needed to maintain these programs.

Increased life expectancy of retirees also adds to the cost of these programs. According to the 2000 U.S. Census, there was a 12% increase in people 65 years of age or older during that decade from 1990 to 2000. It is estimated that by 2040, the elderly population will represent 20.7% of the total population. The largest segment of the population that grew the fastest were people between the ages of 90 and 94, which increased 44.6% since 1990.[4] Overall, the number of people between the ages of 80 and 94 increased 25.7% since 1990.[5] A 65-year-old woman in the U.S., as of the year 2000, could expect to live another 19.2 years and a 65-year old man could expect to live another 16.3 years. In 1900, the average life expectancy was 47.3 years.[6]

This shift in the demographics creates other problems we must face. As elderly people retire, they have a tendency to shift their investments from stocks to more secure positions. Alan Greenspan addressed this issue in February 2002.[7] If retirees move to more secure investments, it leaves only one-third of the now-working population to buy the stocks being sold off. The problem is, when there are more stocks to sell than buyers to buy them, prices fall. Future retirement accounts could plummet again. Compounding this problem is the fact that companies rely on stock revenues for future research and development. This loss of revenue could stifle future economic growth and profits. Relying only on stocks for retirement could result in unintended consequences, caused by

---

[4] http://www.census.gov.
[5] *Id.*
[6] http://www.cdc.gov/nchs/fastats.
[7] Remarks by Alan Greenspan, *Saving for Retirement*, at the 2002 National Summit of Retirement Savings, Department of Labor, Washington, D.C., February 28, 2002.

taxation, unstable market conditions, and the inability to maintain the value in stocks as we now know them.

The Impact of So-called Financial Knowledge

Even with the record number of financial professionals serving the public today, the financial well-being of the American people is on a collision course with disaster. The belief that you can borrow your way to prosperity is rampant. All the financial information given to the public over the last ten years has resulted in record amounts of personal debt, credit card debt, mortgage debt, and personal bankruptcies. The people involved in these problems are the same people we are relying on to fuel the government's future economy and the benefits it provides.

Right now, the public is transferring away more of its earned dollars to interest and taxes than to food, clothing, and housing. This has caused the amount of personal savings in America to almost disappear. So, the question must be asked: Has financial planning, the way it has been sold to the public, done more harm than good?

Not only is debt strangling the American public, but also the cost of living could serve as the straw that breaks the camel's back. Increases in costs and taxes have grown tremendously faster than national incomes. One may argue that we have experienced great growth in our standard of living. But this growth has been driven by record amounts of debt. These are all transfers of our wealth.

Man the Lifeboats

The debt problem will continue to grow. When the government overspends, which has been going on for about 75 years, its problems are passed on to us in the form of more or higher taxes and reduced benefits. The government's solution is simple. When businesses overspend or their costs increase because of material costs, government regulation, increase in corporate taxes, labor, etc., the increases are passed on to us in the form of higher prices. Their solution is simple as well.

When families overspend or their costs increase, the solution is not so simple. The only way to absorb these increases is to reduce their standard of living and spend less money, or go deeper into debt. This is a lose-lose situation. If they spend less, it stifles the economy. If they go deeper into debt, the debt alone will stifle growth and personal savings and a new cycle is created. The government, seeing less revenue coming in because of less spending, seeks new ways (i.e. fees, taxes, regulations) to increase its revenue flow, which is, directly or indirectly, passed on to the public. All of this creates more transfers of our wealth now, and increased transfers in the future. This is a certainty!

Along with shifting age demographics, the government itself plays a role in diminishing our future wealth. Over the last 30 years, the only thing the government has done consistently is overspend the amount of money it has taken in. The government's central focus has become collecting revenues, a/k/a taxes. The government is very good at it, but the financial burdens are passed on to us. We are expected to follow the 47,000 pages of tax law under the threat of penalty or imprisonment. Another problem is that, in 3,000 days, there will be fewer workers to pay for the government's increases in spending, along with the cost of social programs. This will leave an enormous cost burden for the workers to pay, along with the challenge of trying to improve their own standard of living. Diminishing benefits and increasing costs will leave no one satisfied. To survive, the government will have to raise taxes.

I'll Gladly Pay You Tuesday for a Hamburger Today

I think it is important to understand how the government gets its money. We must ask some basic questions. Can the government print and circulate its own money? The answer is NO! Fiat money is money that is not backed by gold or silver. The 10th Amendment of the U.S. Constitution prohibits the printing of fiat money. Next question: Is the Federal Reserve a part of the Federal Government? The answer is NO! The Federal Reserve represents the banks of the United States, and was originally formed to obtain a franchise to create money out of nothing for the purpose of lending.[8] It has been given the power by the government to print fiat money as our currency. Why would the Federal Reserve (banks) want to do this? The Federal Reserve charges interest on the money it prints and loans to the Federal Government. As every good banker knows, a debtor needs income to repay its loan. That is why the government created the 16th Amendment to the U.S. Constitution: to impose an income tax on American citizens. It is interesting that the government tried to impose an income tax on its citizens back in the 1890s only to have the U.S. Supreme Court strike the measure down as unconstitutional. Now, the government receives income from the taxes it collects to repay the loans and interest to the Federal Reserve. This action, in a way, short-circuited the 10th Amendment.

As an example, try to imagine this . . . right after the attacks on September 11, 2001, the government was in desperate need of $60 billion

---

[8] Griffin, G. Edward. *The Creature from Jekyll Island*, American Media, 1994.

dollars. It needed this money to increase security, help clean up New York and the Pentagon, and to support the airline industry. I know this will sound simplistic, but what happened next went something like this . . . The President called Alan Greenspan, the Chair of the Federal Reserve, and asked for $60 billion. Alan ran downstairs and printed $60 billion. He delivered it to the Federal Government at what cost to the Federal Reserve? Almost NOTHING! The government distributed the money to New York, the Pentagon, and the airline industry at what cost to the government? Once again, almost nothing. The cost of all this debt was passed on to us in the form of more debt, higher taxes, and reduced public benefits. Today, we pay anywhere from $330 to $350 billion per year in just interest on the government's debt.

As you can see, the real power of the government is to borrow money and spend it. Unfortunately, it spends much more than the revenue (taxes) it takes in to pay down the loans. There might be confusion when you hear the words government debt and government deficit. A deficit is created when the government overspends its annual budget. The government debt is the accumulated debt of the country from these unpaid deficits. One might conclude that the real problem is that the government spends too much.

To create debt, someone must give you money you haven't earned. Just look at these numbers!

09/10/2008	$9,684,792,611,504.77
09/21/2007	$8,989,952,783,317.53
08/21/2006	$8,503,230,761,750.97
09/30/2005	$7,932,709,661,723.50
09/30/2004	$7,379,052,696,330.32
09/30/2003	$6,783,231,062,743.62
09/30/2002	$6,228,235,965,597.16
09/28/2001	$5,807,463,412,200.06
09/29/2000	$5,674,178,209,886.86
09/30/1999	$5,656,270,901,615.43
09/30/1998	$5,526,193,008,897.62
09/30/1997	$5,413,146,011,397.34
09/30/1996	$5,224,810,939,135.73
09/29/1995	$4,973,982,900,709.39
09/30/1994	$4,692,749,910,013.32
09/30/1993	$4,411,488,883,139.38
09/30/1992	$4,064,620,655,521.66
09/30/1991	$3,665,303,351,697.03
09/28/1990	$3,233,313,451,777.25
09/29/1989	$2,857,430,960,187.32
09/30/1988	$2,602,337,712,041.16
09/30/1987	$2,350,276,890,953.00[9]

---

[9] http://www.treasurydirect.gov/NP/BPDLogin?application=np.

This is the debt of the federal government, and this is a serious problem. Not one year in the last 50 years has this debt gone down. NOT ONE! Politicians claimed record surpluses in the late 1990s and early 2000s, then blamed other politicians when those surpluses had somehow allegedly been lost. How could there be record surpluses and yet no reduction in the debt? These debt numbers are from the government's own web sites. Someone is not telling the truth!

The debt is now everyone's problem. The share of every man, woman, and child in America has grown and will continue to grow significantly. Even with record amounts of revenue being collected in the form of taxes, the debt continues to grow. Along with the debt and the government's continuous overspending, the cost of social programs also continues to grow. These programs will have a record number of participants with longer life expectancies, all at much greater costs in the very near future.

It should be a mystery to no one why the government continues to overspend its budgets. It suffers from a lack of fiscal discipline, and it has the ability to borrow money whenever it wants to— this is a dangerous combination, given its history. Day after day, the problem escalates. The government continues to increase its spending and the population gets older. Due to the demographic shifts alone, the costs of government social programs will double in the next 20 years. This is a certainty!

With a smaller workforce, more productivity will be needed from fewer workers to support an ever-growing retired population. At the same time, the current workforce also strives to increase their standards of living and save for their retirement. The dilemma is clear, and the solution to this dilemma does not yet exist. Things must change.

Sustaining the Unsustainable

Sustaining the Unsustainable

In the event of an approaching dangerous storm, it is imperative that one makes the necessary preparations in order to avoid disaster. Knowing what is about to happen and what to do before it happens is crucial. This is true of your financial world also. When it is evident that financial storm clouds are approaching, you must already be prepared. It wasn't raining when Noah started building the ark. Preparing for the storm after it has started may be too late. Unfortunately, even being prepared for a storm that is coming will not stop the storm. Those who aren't ready for this event will be surprised and shocked that they have become victims of the storm.

Sustaining the Unsustainable:
The Horizon

Off in the distance, there are definite signs that something is happening, and it does not look good. Financially speaking, the horizon is darkening quickly even though the sun is still shining now. The trouble that is brewing is man-made and out of control, and no one should expect it to just go away. The core of this financial storm has a powerful center and continues to grow. It <u>is</u>

coming. Here is what is at the center of this storm.

As I mentioned earlier, last year in the United States there was an increase in credit expansion of $2,718 billion. This tremendous increase in credit occurred during the same period when inflation-adjusted incomes did NOT rise and there was NO increase in personal savings. The euphoria over our economic growth is silenced when we learn that it is being driven by debt. This phenomenon has been occurring now for about 15 years. The government debt (not deficit) alone is about $10 trillion. Sixty-six percent of this debt has come into being since 1990.[10] Alarmingly, just the interest on the government's debt is $41 MILLION DOLLARS PER HOUR, every hour of the day, seven days a week. In perspective, this interest payment comes to about $690,000 per minute or about $11,500 per second.[11] This amount is devastating and continues to grow every day, out of control. Remember, the fact is, over the past 50 years, the government debt, on an annual basis, has NEVER gone down. This information can be found on the government's own web sites.[12]

Even though the government recognizes this debt problem, they continue to spend about $1.35 for every $1.00 they collect in tax revenues. It would be logical to assume that to raise revenue to

---

[10] http://mwhodges.home.att.net.
[11] http://www.brillig.com/debt_clock.
[12] http://www.treasurydirect.gov/NP/BPDLogin?application=np.

pay off this debt and still operate the country, the government MUST raise taxes. They know it; you know it; I know it.

The debt situation is just one cloud on the horizon, but it's a big one. Even more concerning is this problem: The future financial liabilities of the federal government totals about $50 trillion. Now, I want you to be sitting down when you read this. That $50 trillion dollars of debt is three times the amount of money in circulation in the entire world!

A Cup of Truth,
Half a Cup of Reality,
and the Government

The average American can sense the seriousness of the situation, yet preparing for these events is curiously a distant option. The problem is that the government continues to assure future generations of retirement benefits, and makes promises that cannot be kept. The "now" working generation has paid so little to finance these future obligations that even the most prosperous economy in history could not pay the bill.

The Government's Cost
for the Average American

Take a look at an average American couple, who earned the average income during their lives and retired at the age of 65. Together, they earned about $47,000 in their final year of work. They would receive a joint Medicare benefit valued at $283,500.[13] The reality is, they would have paid only $43,000 in Medicare taxes during their working years. This represents a $240,000 loss to the government. Remember, this is only ONE husband and wife.

The government's problem with the average 65-year-old retiree doesn't end there. Although this average couple paid $198,000 in Social Security taxes, longer life expectancies will create an average $326,000 in Social Security benefits for this couple. Between Medicare and Social Security, the government, for this average couple, paid out $368,000 more in benefits at retirement than the couple paid in. To make things worse, the benefits for these programs increase every year. Finally, the Social Security and Medicare trust funds have no money in them, only IOUs that future taxpayers must pay.[14]

---

[13] "The Looming National Benefit Crisis," by Dennis Cauchon and John Waggoner, *USA Today*, October 3, 2004.
[14] "Truth and Transparency: The Federal Government's Financial Condition and Fiscal Outlook," by Hon. David M. Walker, *Journal of Accountancy*, April 2004.

Unfortunately, the children of this average couple, who are 40 to 45 years old, now will receive projected benefits 45% higher than their parents, costing the government about $884,000 when they turn 65.

No one should expect this problem to go away. The changing demographics are certain to happen. The questions remain: Who will pay for this, and how much will future taxation have to increase to maintain these benefits?

> *"No one should expect productivity growth to be sufficient to bail us out. . . Ensuring fiscal stability would require an overall federal tax burden well above its long-term average."* Remarks by Alan Greenspan at the 2002 National Summit of Retirement Savings, Department of Labor, Washington, D.C., February 28, 2002.

Someone must pay all of this debt. If you're guessing it's you and me and people who haven't been born yet, you're right. But our ability to pay down this debt is a problem and is compounded by the fact that inflation-adjusted personal incomes for the average male have NOT gone up in the last 25 years. In 2004, real incomes for the average male actually went down. One must conclude a larger percentage of one's income will go to paying off government and personal debt. Those amounts continue to rise every year whether personal incomes rise or not.

Maintaining a standard of living has also become more difficult and affects one's ability to save and grow wealth. The cost of owning and maintaining a home has grown faster than personal incomes. As a percentage, property taxes have grown faster than incomes. The cost of health care has tremendously outpaced personal incomes. Increases in college education costs have grown faster than personal inflation-adjusted incomes. The increase in the cost of gas, heating oil, utilities, etc. have all exceeded the growth of personal incomes. The cost of the federal government has increased 42% faster than incomes, and the cost of state government has increased 168% faster than national income averages.[15] Government regulations, fees, and taxes on corporations all impact the prices of goods and services you receive. A simple example of this would be the government raising the fees or changing the corporate regulations on bread manufacturers. The fees or regulation costs are passed on to the consumer: you and me. The bread people, not wanting to raise the price of a loaf of bread because the consumer would notice, simply take two pieces of bread out of the loaf. No matter what, the cost continues to grow.

Evidence of the strain being put on individual incomes by personal and government debt is clear. More money allocated for debt and interest has

---

[15] "The Looming National Benefit Crisis," by Dennis Cauchon and John Waggoner, *USA Today*, October 3, 2004.

impacted everyone's ability to save money. According to the Bureau of Economic Analysis (BEA), personal savings in the United States is down 100% over the last 20 years.[16] According to the BEA's studies, the average Americans' savings have all but disappeared.[17] Personal savings rates or, should we say, someone's ability to save has not been this low since the 1930s during the Great Depression.[18] This inability to save creates darkness on the horizon and adds depth to the storm's seriousness.

Let's scan the horizon now. What do we see? GROWING GOVERNMENT DEBT - a dark cloud. GROWING PERSONAL DEBT - a dark cloud. INTEREST ON THIS DEBT - a dark cloud. ADJUSTED INCOMES ARE FLAT - a dark cloud. RECORD CREDIT EXPANSION - a dark cloud. LOWEST SAVINGS SINCE 1930 - a dark cloud. INCREASING COST OF LIVING - a dark cloud.

Some may try to convince you that this financial horizon will create only a shower or two. Beware! What we have just discussed in this section thus far are not projections that might happen in the future; these events are happening RIGHT NOW, and no one can deny it. But now it is my job to show you what is behind the first line of storm clouds to give you a better view of how this will

---

[16] http://www.bea.gov.
[17] *Id.*
[18] *Id.*

impact your future.

Sustaining the Unsustainable: Beyond the Horizon

Looking beyond what we can see right now, the forecast becomes disturbing. The shifting demographics will intensify conditions dramatically. It is ironic that some people choose to continue following the advice of those who have created, and continue to create, the problems we are facing. Financially, the cost of sustaining the ever-growing aging population with the promised government benefits will drain almost all our financial resources. But the government continues to believe that it can borrow its way to prosperity. Unfortunately, many people have followed the same philosophy in their own personal lives. The government, so desperate to convince the public that everything will be okay, is now using the calculation of future revenues that they will receive from people who have not even been born yet. I can see it now—a birth tax. During the Cold War between the U.S.S.R. and the United States, victory became ours when the U.S.S.R. spent itself out of existence. Now, I fear, our own government is doing the same thing to itself. The burden of cleaning up and rebuilding from the damage created by this storm will fall on the backs of all of us: the taxpayers. What will intensify the dark clouds of this coming storm on the horizon are the changing demographics. For certain, the second wave of this storm is going to happen, and these changes are more dramatic than we can even imagine.

Sustaining the Unsustainable: The Government Prepares Itself for the Storm

So clear are the signs of the danger from this storm and the certainty that it is going to happen, you only need to take notice of changes the government is making to help it survive the oncoming storm. The government understands the statistics and demographics better than anyone and continues to try to sustain the unsustainable. But, behind the scenes, the government is preparing.

QUALIFIED PLAN CHANGES. Recently, the government made changes to the amounts that you can deposit on an annual basis into 401(k) programs and IRAs.[19] On the surface, this appears to be a benefit to everyone who is involved in one of these programs. But, if you study this more carefully and confirm this with some basic math, you may come to the conclusion that there is more of a benefit to the government than there is to you. They know,

---

[19] http://www.irs.gov/publications/p525.

because of the demographic shifts, as a percentage, there will be more retirees and fewer taxpaying workers. The government needs larger pools of money from these fewer workers to tax, at whatever rate they can, to secure greater future tax revenues. Remember, these plans were sold to you as a tax savings.

THE CATCH-UP PROVISION. Not only did the government increase the amount you can put into qualified plans, but also, if you are of a certain age, you can put an additional amount into qualified plans to "help" you "save" for retirement.[20] But, before you run off and do this, let's take a deeper look. If someone puts $5,000 per year into a qualified plan for 10 years, for a total of $50,000, and they thought they could receive a 6% rate of return on this money during those 10 years, what would be their share if they retired to a 30% tax bracket? $48,300. Remember, they put in $50,000.

SOCIAL SECURITY. This program should be renamed Social Insecurity. The government continues to tweak the ages when someone can receive full benefits that they paid for or, in some cases, that they didn't pay for. With life expectancies of people reaching into their eighties and nineties, the government seeks to save some money by

---

[20] http://www.irs.gov/publications/p553.

increasing the age one must be to receive full benefits.[21]

BANKRUPTCY LAWS. The government knows, since they are the experts on debt, that more and more people are drowning financially because of the tremendous amounts of personal debt. Recently, the government prided itself on the fact that personal bankruptcies leveled off at about 1,700,000 filings per year. A closer look would tell you, if that number is the average for 10 years, that means over 6% of our total population filed for bankruptcy protection. Now, the new bankruptcy laws do not totally forgive the debt of certain filers, and payments must be made on that debt into the future.[22] Of course, any taxes due in this bankruptcy must be paid in full with interest.

MORTGAGES. Recently, 40-year government-sponsored mortgages were re-introduced.[23] Why, you might ask. How would this benefit the government? The politician would have you believe it's to help you buy a nicer house, but the real reason involves a little deeper thought process. You

---

[21] "In Brief: Increasing the Age of Eligibility for Social Security and Medicare," by D. Wittenberg, D. Stapleton and S. Scrivener, *Social Security Bulletin*, September 2000.

[22] "Law changes spur bankruptcy filings," by David Carpenter, *USA Today*, September 23, 2005.

[23] "40 year mortgages hit the mainstream," by Bankrate.com, http://moneycentral.msn.com, June 14, 2005.

see, buying a home is determined on how much you can afford to pay on a monthly basis. If you lengthen the mortgage years, you can afford a more expensive house. The government NEEDS to maintain the values of these properties as high as they can because these values are taxed. Think of the 40-year mortgage as putting you deeper into debt, so you can pay higher taxes. The government is very fearful of housing prices going down, since it is a source of tax revenue.

As a side note to this, it seems as if property values go up every year, increasing the property taxes accordingly. If housing prices went down, how long do you think it will take the government to reduce those taxes? FOREVER. That is, IF they ever reduce them at all.

Failure of the housing market would trigger a record number of foreclosures and cause financial and economic disaster. For years, the Federal Reserve, with the encouragement of the Federal Government, has granted loans in the form of mortgages to people who really don't qualify for these loans. It could be only a matter of time that this situation may cause an economic disaster that the government or financial institutions would not be able to survive. If this crisis were to happen, be leery of government solutions. We may end up paying for all the mistakes they have made. Their solution will have us pay for their mistakes while they still collect a record amount of taxes. They win.

REVERSE MORTGAGES. The government also introduced reverse mortgages for people over the age of 62.[24] Because of increasing life expectancies and people outliving their retirement savings, this mortgage allows retirees to withdraw the values of their homes to support their incomes. The government, understanding that full impact of demographic changes are coming, needed to do this to take the pressure off itself of having to raise and increase the benefits they provide. The funny thing is, when reverse mortgages were first introduced years ago, the government considered them risky. I guess the government finally figured out that as long as the risk is borne by someone else, it's okay.

EMINENT DOMAIN. A recent challenge against eminent domain was struck down by the Supreme Court of the United States.[25] This decision allows Federal, State, and Local governments to seize and take control of property, any property, under the premise that taking this property will benefit the general public. Who determines what will benefit the general public will be a problem. But the government profiting from these takeovers won't.

---

[24] http://www.fha-home-loans.com/reverse_mortgage.htm.
[25] Kelo, et al. v. New London, et al. (04-108), 268 Conn. 1, 843 A. 2d 500, affirmed (2005).

GOVERNMENT SOLVENCY. Knowing full well of the challenges that are coming, the government has positioned itself as the "save all cure all" safety net for businesses, banks, and other financial institutions. Don't be alarmed, but the government solution to any disaster is you, the taxpayer. Watch for increasing government control in different sectors of the economy. It will signal the beginning of the end to everyone's financial freedom.

The steps the government is beginning to take confirm the coming problems. The warnings by the government officials of doubling taxes and decreasing benefits by 50% are lightning strikes in our financial futures. The changes the government must make are just beginning. To verify the seriousness of this approaching storm, take a look at speeches made by David Walker, former Comptroller General of the United States, head of the Government Accountability Office (GAO). Specifically, take a look at "Truth and Transparency: The Federal Government's Financial Condition and Fiscal Outlook," an address delivered by Hon. David M. Walker to the National Press Club in Washington, D.C., on September 17, 2003.

Sustaining the Unsustainable:
Surviving the Storm

You cannot be aware of something you're not aware of. On the streets, American life goes on one day at a time, unaware of the uncertain future. People are aware that their paychecks are not increasing as fast as the price of housing, property taxes, health care, education, gas, utilities, insurance, etc., so adjustments are made by saving less and increasing their debt a little. The financial advice they receive is equivalent to nothing more than buying an umbrella to prepare for a hurricane. Add to this the fact that the government's failure to reduce its spending increases its urgency to raise taxes in the very near future. This action will further drain personal incomes. This storm is coming.

The most important thing you can do to prepare for these events is to KNOW, beforehand, that these events are going to happen. Your newfound awareness will help you to prepare, as the answers can be found inside the problem itself. All of the solutions in preparation for your financial future should have four goals in mind:

1. These solutions should increase your money supply now and in the future.
2. These solutions should create more or better benefits for you.

3.   These solutions should reduce the amount of risk and taxation you are exposed to.

4.   These solutions should cost you no additional money than you are already spending.

Now, as we mentioned earlier, everyone is involved in transfers of their wealth. The transfers are taxes, tax refunds, qualified plans, owning a home, investments, life insurance, disability, owning a car, credit cards, and financial planning.

Most people unknowingly and unnecessarily transfer away a great deal of money on the aforementioned transfers. Recapturing this transferred money is important. By doing this, you will increase your money supply. Having more money will be a benefit to you. No risk on your part will be involved, and you will not spend one more dime than you are already spending to do this. Although recapturing these transfers sounds difficult, it's NOT. It would be my recommendation though that you find a skilled professional who is trained to guide you through these transfers. This person should also teach you and educate you, not simply sell you another product. Having more knowledge to make better decisions will help you prepare for the coming financial storm.

Once you learn how to recapture these transfers, you will increase your money supply. Since we are all aware that, in the near future, taxes must and will go up, it will be important not to involve your money in vehicles where it will be taxed now or in the future. Future taxation will be devastating to your money supply. Modern-day thinkers will have you believe that your money portfolio should be based on the proper balance of investments. The reality is, your portfolio should be centrally focused on future taxes: the number-one transfer of your wealth. As an example, let's say a person retired on $100,000 per year in a 30% tax bracket. This person would have $70,000 to live on after giving $30,000 to the IRS for income taxes. Imagine now if this person had retired with a retirement portfolio that had been designed to have the least tax exposure, instead of a fully taxable portfolio. If this person's portfolio was 50% taxable and 50% tax-free at retirement, he or she could blend these two for an income of $100,000, with a tax bill of only $15,000 instead of $30,000 every year. Now imagine how the first person we discussed would feel if taxes went up in the future. Now change that last sentence from "if taxes go up" to "when taxes go up." That storm is coming. Prepare properly.

Sustaining the Unsustainable

Every aspect of your financial future will be shaped by the changing future events. The horizon is filled with uncertainty and danger. I identified some of the storm clouds earlier. Here are the coming storm's dangerous components.

•Continuing record government spending
•Growing government debt
•Growing personal debt
•Stagnant inflation-adjusted incomes
•Rising interest on government and personal debt
•Record amount of credit expansion
•Decreasing personal savings
•Increasing cost of living
•Decreasing standard of living
•Increasing future taxation
•Decreasing government benefits
•Tremendous demographic changes
•Rising costs of war, terror, security, and disasters

The current status quo of the government will be unable to survive the elements of this storm. The victims, you and I, will not be in a position to ride out the storm if we continue to follow traditional thinking.

Electing the Unelectable

In order to confront these changes and start to rebuild our society, strong leadership is needed. And the certainty is that someone running on a platform to get elected, and laying out to the public the changes that would be necessary to fix the mess we are in, wouldn't receive a single vote in the election. Imagine this. . .

"My fellow Americans, today I'm announcing my candidacy and that I hope to be elected President of the United States. We are headed down a path that is unclear, uncertain, and dangerous. We have been put in a position, by the last six decades of elected officials, of possibly having to watch the country collapse completely. The trouble is upon us now, and we are unprepared for its future. We will fail if certain decisions are not made.

"First of all, my fellow Americans, in order to survive, everyone, rich and poor, will have to pay 35% in income taxes. I also will recommend eliminating all deductions on income taxes. It will also be necessary to eliminate Medicare and Medicaid. This will help preserve the promises we have made regarding the Social Security program for a future generation. To help cut costs in the medical industry, we will also eliminate all medical lawsuits except for gross negligence. I will eliminate the capital gains tax because, as you can see, you're going to have to fend for yourself and your family.

"My platform also includes eliminating the government's pension insurance business. Companies should be liable to their employees for their own retirement plans. I will eliminate FEMA and give back to the state the responsibility of caring for its citizens. From now on, no new taxes can be implemented without a vote of the public. I will also eliminate any pork-barreling measures attached to any new bills. It is my goal to eliminate the two-party political system and eliminate all pensions for state and federal employees and elected officials.

"I also believe any elected official that is caught overspending or voting to overspend any budget set forth at any level of government (local, state, or federal) should be banned from voting on any legislation or bill during their remaining time in office and then not be allowed to run for re-election. It is simply a matter of fiduciary trust.

"The Federal Government will only provide 1) security and protection for its citizens, 2) a strong military, 3) tax collection and distribution of 75% of that money to the states where it came from, and 4) the country's transportation infrastructure. Additionally, everyone on government assistance must do six weeks of service or training per year, while they are on assistance, to their state's National Guard or parks services until they reach the age of 65 or stop receiving assistance.

"I would also eliminate frivolous lawsuits by establishing a 'winner takes all' rule. If someone sues you for $1,000,000, and they lose, they owe you the million dollars. This will save our court systems billions of dollars.

"To bring back some sense of civility in the political arena, rather than allow politicians to spread hate and have this hate overflow to the public, I will allow dueling between political members whose righteous beliefs need defending. I believe these duels should be publicized and televised, with the revenues from these programs going towards reducing our debt.

"Finally, there is a harsh reality in life. We are not victims of our society that have to be coddled. Grow up, take responsibility, stop looking for your 15 minutes of fame, become a productive member of a society that we all want, and develop pride in a legacy that you will leave behind. Vote for me."

The reality is, what we need is for the government to straighten out the mess they have created, but no one has the political courage to do it. The problem is that no one would vote for someone who promised to raise taxes, to cut or eliminate government benefits and programs, and that everyone would suffer financially. The thing is, if we are going to survive as a country, this is what we need to happen.

Thinking the Unthinkable: Social Insecurity

The crown jewel of the government's social programs is Social Security. The joke for the average American is that Social Security will probably not be around when they retire. Politicians have been put in charge of this sacred promise to the people and, in their own words, they are protecting, guarding, and preserving these future benefits. You are led to believe that the money that is coming out of your paycheck is put in trust for safekeeping. But, another storm is brewing.

"Trust Fund balances are available to finance future benefits...but only in a bookkeeping sense...they do not consist of real economic assets that can be drawn down in the future to fund benefits. Instead, they are claims on the Treasury that, when redeemed, will have to be financed by raising taxes or borrowing." President Bill Clinton in his Analytical Perspectives section of the 2000 budget.

"It holds no real assets. Consequently, it does not generate funds to pay future benefits. These so-called trust fund 'assets' simply reflect the accumulated sum of funds transferred from Social Security over the years to finance other government operations." June O'Neill, former Director of the Congressional Budget Office (CBO), at the CATO Institute's Conference for Women and Social Security.

"You know, one thing about Social Security—sorry to blow on here, but now that you asked—a lot of people in America think there is a trust. Your money goes in, the government holds it, and then the government gives your money back when you retire. That's just not the way it works. And it's important for the American citizens to understand it's a pay-as-you-go system. And right now, we're paying for a lot of programs other than Social Security with the payroll tax coming in, thereby leaving a pile of IOUs." George W. Bush in a press conference on March 16, 2005.

"We have no positive assets in the Social Security Trust Fund." Secretary of the Treasury, and one of the trustees, Paul O'Neill, June 19, 2001, at a luncheon speech to the Coalition for American Financial Security in the Sky Room of the World Trade Center and later to Sam Donaldson on *This Week,* Sunday, June 25, 2001.

"Government trust funds do not correspond in any meaningful way to those in the private sector. Government trust funds are simply a form of earmarking, accounting mechanisms that record tax receipts, user fees, and other credits and associated expenditures." Barry Anderson of the Congressional Budget Office in testimony before the House Budget Committee, September 2002.

"We are going to get no help from the so-called Social Security Trust Fund. The Fund is a collection of non-negotiable government bonds in a filing cabinet in West Virginia. Investing in Treasury certificates is a good idea unless you are the Treasury. The idea that somehow this represents anything other than records kept on money collected by Social Security taxes that had been spent on other programs in the last 20 years is a complete fraud. When the president talks about using the Trust Fund to extend the life of the Social Security program for 24 years, he is wrong. We are misleading people into thinking that this Trust Fund has any relevance whatsoever. From an economic

and a legal point of view, there is no Trust Fund." Former Senator Phil Gramm, at the Economic Club of New York.

"In fact, the money the government has supposedly been putting aside from the Baby Boomers' Social Security taxes is not there. The government has been borrowing the money to pay for the budget deficit. The Social Security Trust Fund is simply IOUs from the U.S. Treasury.... [Social Security] would be fine if the government would stop borrowing the money." Newt Gingrich, April 7, 1995.

"The Enron case made headlines because fraud and deception of such magnitude is fairly unusual in the corporate world. Washington fraud and deception of a much greater magnitude doesn't make the headlines because fraud and deception in government is standard practice....Washington politicians have for decades been doing precisely what Enron has been accused of doing—concealing debt with accounting tricks. Congressmen tell us that our Social Security taxes go into a trust fund to pay for future retirement pensions. That is a boldface lie. The Social Security trust fund has no money in it." Walter Williams, Professor of Economics, George Mason University in an article published by the *Washington Times,* April 17, 2002.

"It means that ordinary working Americans, like teachers, police officers, and firefighters, who

believe their payroll taxes are going toward their Social Security retirement are in for a surprise... Instead of going to the Social Security trust fund, their payroll contributions are being funneled directly into tax breaks for individuals and corporations." Robert Matsui (D-CA), Chairman House Ways & Means Subcommittee on Social Security, Associated Press, March 30, 2002.

"The Social Security trust fund is what I call a fiscal oxymoron. It shouldn't be trusted, and it's not funded. And whether you have one or not, you still have to go out and do the same three things. You either have to try to borrow the money or you're going to increase taxes or you are going to cut the benefits. We've spent the money in the trust fund. We may have told the American people that we were setting it aside in a quote 'trust fund.' We spent it on other subjects. Shock of all shocks." Pete Peterson, head of the Concord Coalition and former Commerce Secretary, January 13, 2005.

"The biggest lie that is being told in this whole thing—and it is a lie—is that there is plenty of money in the Social Security Trust Fund to carry this thing through to 2050. It's a lie. There is no money in the trust fund." Representative E. Clay Shaw, Jr. (R-FL) House Ways & Means Subcommittee on Social Security, interviewed by Doug Lyons for the *Sun Sentinel*, February 13, 2005.

It seems that the politicians are playing Russian roulette with our future. The demographic changes in the next 3,000 days will greatly increase the number of people in the Social Security program. This is compounded by the fact that people in the Social Security program are living much longer. Also, the government has promised cost of living increases in these benefits every year. No matter what political spin you put on Social Security, if you use logic to try to sustain the unsustainable, the outlook is bleak. We are now forced to think the unthinkable.

At War with the Future

Once again, knowing what and when events are going to take place in the near future and how they will impact your life is essential. When it comes to your finances, having this type of information is critical. According to David Walker, former Comptroller General of the United States and head of the General Accountability Office (GAO), to balance the budget by 2014, taxes on corporate and individual incomes would have to increase by 38%.[26] If taxes are not increased, then Social Security and Medicare would have to be cut

---

[26] "Truth and Transparency: The Federal Government's Financial Condition and Fiscal Outlook," by Hon. David M. Walker, *Journal of Accountancy*, April 2004.

by 55%.[27] The demographic shifts that ARE going to take place WILL deteriorate the situation even more. Walker states that if nothing is done by 2030, payroll taxes will have to increase by 100% and income taxes increase by 50%.[28] At that point, if taxes are not increased by those amounts, then Social Security, Medicare, and all non-defense spending would have to be cut in half. Quoting Walker, "Deficits do matter, especially if they are large, structural, and recurring in nature. In addition, our projected budget deficits are not manageable without significant changes in the status quo programs, policies, processes, and operations . . . We cannot simply grow our way out of this problem."[29]

The reason I point this out is that the wisdom of saving money now and deferring the taxes on that money to a later date may cause you great financial harm. The U.S. Treasury Financial Report reported in the fiscal year 2004 that the spending shortages in Social Security and Medicare were eight times the total amount of government spending in fiscal year 2002.[30] That comes to about $200,000 for every household in the United States. That amount of money is about double the value of all the stocks, bonds, and mutual funds that all Americans now own.

---

[27] *Id.*
[28] *Id.*
[29] *Id.*
[30] http://www.fms.treas.gov/fr.

In 1999, I made a decision to become an educational force to make the public aware of the demographic changes and the impact it would have on the economy. I've been traveling across the country for the past several years telling people about the oncoming storm, pointing out the obvious . . . the changing demographics, increasing government spending, the impending Social Security and Medicare crises, the exuberant consumer spending due to the housing bubble, the growing debt and billowing credit expansion in the U.S. As a result of my travels, I met many professionals with similar thoughts, and thus I have formed a group of professionals from across the country who is deeply concerned about the direction we are headed and the impact it will have on everyone's financial future.

It appears now that the knowledge is spreading—that society is finally looking at the horizon with concern.

"We face a 'demographic tsunami' that will never recede," David Walker told a group of reporters. He ran through a long list of fiscal challenges, "led by the imminent retirement of the baby boomers, whose promised Medicare and Social Security benefits will swamp the federal budget in coming decades.[31]

---

[31] "A 'fiscal hurricane' on the horizon," by Richard Wolf, *USA Today,* November 15, 2005.

"Sadly, it's no laughing matter. To hear Walker, the nation's top auditor, tell it, the United States can be likened to Rome before the fall of the empire. Its financial condition is 'worse than advertised,' he says. It has a 'broken business model.' It faces deficits in its budget, its balance of payments, its savings—and its leadership.[32]

"Walker's not the only one saying it. As Congress and the White House struggle to trim up to $50 billion from the federal budget over five years—just 3% of the $1.6 trillion in deficits projected for that period—budget experts say the nation could soon face its worst fiscal crisis since at least 1983, when Social Security bordered on bankruptcy.[33]

"Without major spending cuts, tax increases, or both, the national debt will grow more than $3 trillion through 2010, to $11.2 trillion—nearly $38,000 for every man, woman, and child. The interest alone would cost $561 billion in 2010, the same as the Pentagon.[34]

---

[32] *Id.*
[33] *Id.*
[34] *Id.*

"Douglas Holtz-Eakin, director of the non-partisan Congressional Budget Office, dispassionately arms 535 members of Congress with his agency's stark projections. Barring action, he admits to be 'terrified' about the budget deficit in coming decades. That's when an aging population, health care inflation, and advanced medical technology will create a perfect storm of spiraling costs.[35]

"Maya MacGuineas, president of the bipartisan Committee for a Responsible Federal Budget, sees a future of unfunded promises, trade imbalances, too few workers, and too many retirees. She envisions a stock market dive, lost assets, and a lower standard of living.[36]

"Kent Conrad, a Democratic senator from North Dakota, points to the nation's $7.9 trillion debt, rising by about $600 billion a year. That, he notes, is before the baby boomer retires. 'We're not preparing for what we all know is to come,' he says. 'We're all sleepwalking through this period.'[37]

"Prescription drug coverage under Medicare takes effect Jan. 1. Its projected cost, advertised at $400 billion over 10 years when it passed in 2003, has risen to at least $720 billion. 'We couldn't afford it,' Walker says of the new law.[38]

---

[35] *Id.*
[36] *Id.*
[37] *Id.*
[38] *Id.*

"The leading edge of the baby boom hits age 62 in 2008 and can take early retirement. The number of people covered by Social Security is expected to grow from 47 million today to 69 million in 2020. By 2030, the Congressional Budget Office projects Social Security spending as a share of the U.S. economy will rise by 40%.[39]

"Inaction could have these consequences, experts say: Higher interest rates. Lower wages. Shrinking pensions. Slower economic growth. A lesser standard of living. Higher taxes in the future for today's younger generation. Less savings. More consumption. Plunging stock and bond prices. Recession.[40]

"Walker's agency churns reports with titles such as 'Human Capital: Selected Agencies Have Opportunities to Enhance Existing Succession Planning and Management Efforts.' But he knows he must try to humanize the numbers, and his rhetoric on the nation's fiscal course has become more acerbic. 'Anybody who says you're going to grow your way out of this problem,' Walker says, 'would probably not pass math.'"[41]

---

[39] *Id.*
[40] *Id.*
[41] *Id.*

The collapse of the housing bubble will throw the economy into a recession, and quite likely a severe recession.

"The Center for Economic and Policy Research predicts worse, saying a bubble burst would mean the loss of 5 million to 6.3 million jobs. The housing run up has financed consumer spending, creating more than $5 trillion in bubble wealth, the center estimates. Consumers have used 'cash-out' mortgages to pay for everything from new kitchens to college tuition.[43]

"A final nightmare scenario: A federal bailout of the mortgage market is likely if housing crashes, the center predicts. So, if corporate pension funds continue to falter, and this dire prediction does come true, the Feds could be conceivably holding your mortgage and your pension.[44]

"Another indicator, unsold homes sitting on the market, also points down. The ratio of inventories to sales has been rising rapidly in recent months and now stands at its highest level since 1996, according to Wachovia Corp.[45]

---

[43] *Id.*
[44] *Id.*
[45] *Id.*

"Then there's the problem of affordability. Affordability for first-time buyers is the worst it has been in 20 years, which brings to mind an old parable about the stock market. A woman buys up a company stock, driving up the price as she goes. Eventually, she tells her broker to sell. His response: 'To whom?'"[46]

Don't Worry, Be Happy

Although most political and public talk is centered on the income tax, the government has been busy and very creative inventing new taxes. An example is that there are no less than seven different taxes on the use of a telephone. Stay at a hotel, and there are no less than four taxes for your one-night stay. The list seems to be never-ending. The government continues to collect revenues at a record pace while its debt has grown to an all-time high.

While our eyes are only focused on what is going on with the income tax and decreasing benefits that reduce our paychecks, the other new taxes, or hidden taxes, increase much faster than our incomes rise. The increases in the underlying taxes don't make headlines and go unnoticed by the general public. The increase in these taxes eats away at our standard of living and our ability to save.

---

[46] *Id.*

Although it was deemed unconstitutional in the 1890s, the income tax took effect in 1913. Less than one percent of the population made enough money back then, to be taxed. The 16th Amendment passed easily through Congress because it was thought to be inconsequential. The maximum tax in 1913 was about 7%. During World Wars I and II, the Federal marginal tax brackets soared to almost 90%. The marginal tax brackets remained high, in the 70% and 80% range, right into the mid-1980s. The tax reform acts of the 1980s greatly reduced the Federal marginal tax bracket to 31%, but took away almost all of the deductions one could claim on one's tax return. By doing this, the Federal Government began to collect record amounts of revenue from the public. Then, in the early 1990s, another tax increase was implemented, this time increasing the marginal rate to 39%. One might believe it was only an 8% difference between the two rates, but it was actually about a 28% increase in the tax table. Remember, they had all but eliminated any tax deductions.

The government continues, year after year, to set new records on the amount of tax revenues it collects. To make things worse, the government continues to overspend, in record proportions, the amounts it has taken in. Understanding the demographics of the country will compound this problem, and taxes will have to be continually increased. It's a certainty.

Old Wise Tales

The current financial wisdom that will trample your future is this: You will probably retire to two-thirds of your income, thus be in a lower tax bracket. This misunderstanding is older than dirt. I came across my father's 1960 tax return; he, too, was given this wisdom. In 1960, the Federal marginal tax bracket was near 80%, but my father was allowed to deduct everything he bought. His realized tax bracket in 1960, after deductions, was 12%. Twenty-five years later, he did retire to two-thirds of his income, but he retired to a 28% tax bracket. Now, 12% to 28% is not just a 16% increase. It equates to a 140% increase in the tax table. No wonder public sentiment toward the government grows negative and suspicious when they discover how much of their earnings are being eaten away.

The government contests they are looking out for our best interests. If it were truly concerned, don't you think the government would sponsor infomercials on how to eliminate or reduce your taxes? Not a chance. If it were really concerned, why not just lower taxes and eliminate or reduce government spending?

Another misconception is that a tax refund is a great thing. The first thing you have to do upon having received a refund is admit that you made a mistake. You overpaid for something and didn't get your money back for a year. Don't act as if it were a victory over the IRS. It wasn't. You overpaid. What interest did they pay you for the use of your money all year? Zero percent. In fact, you may have had to hire someone, an accountant or CPA, to help you get back something that was already yours. The average refund is almost enough to make your car payments throughout the year. A refund is a foolish transfer of your money.

The
Landscape
of
America

In the Land of Oz

I have found, in my travels across the country, that many people have some things in common. The average refund per taxpayer is about $3,000. This same typical American may have about $150,000 in his (or her) 401(k). The average person also owns a home. In that home, let's say this person has about $100,000 in equity. The average person may also have some other investments other than his 401(k). This would be mutual funds or stocks. Let's assume he has $20,000 in such accounts. It would not be uncommon for this person to have $10,000 in a bank savings account as well. So, the summary of this person's finances might look a little like the following.

$3,000	Annual tax refund
$150,000	401(k)
$100,000	Equity in home
$20,000	Investment funds (IF)
$10,000	Bank savings (BS)

All of this looks pretty normal for an average person. You might even say that, depending on this person's age, they are doing pretty well. But, let's take a deeper look at what is really happening here to the average American in this situation. Let's start with that average annual tax refund. Again, what is the rate of return on that refund? The government has had your money all year; they must be crediting you interest for having the use of your money, right? Wrong! Your refund carries a zero percent rate of return on it.

Now, let's take a look at this person's $150,000 in their 401(k). What would you say has been the average annual rate of return on this account over the past seven years? Remember, the events of September 11, 2001 may still have these accounts in negative numbers. But, let's try to be positive and say this account has earned an average of 6% per year.

Let's now look at this person's $100,000 of equity he has in his home. Once again, what's the rate of return on this $100,000? It's zero percent. You see, the value of your home rises or falls, regardless of how much equity you have in it.

As for this person's investment funds (IF) of $20,000, much like the returns in the 401(k), many of these accounts have had trouble getting back to the values they were at six or seven years ago. Let's just say this account also averages 6% per year. And then there is that fabulous bank savings account of $10,000. What's the typical rate of return on that money? One or two percent if you're lucky, so let's just give it a 1.5% rate of return.

Now, let's summarize this person's accounts

again.

$3,000	Annual tax refund	0% rate of return
$150,000	401(k)	6% rate of return
$100,000	Equity in home	0% rate of return
$20,000	Investment funds (IF)	6% rate of return
$10,000	Bank savings (BS)	1.5% rate of return

Take a step back and look at this for a second. How does it look now with the rates of return added in? Not all that terrific. Yet, we are not done. There is another issue we must address with these accounts, and it's called taxes.

Are there taxes on that annual tax refund of $3,000? In most cases the answer is no. Will the 401(k) be taxed? Yes, when you start taking the money out of it. Is the equity in your home taxed? In most cases, under current law, the answer is no. Will the gains in that investment account (IF) be taxed? Of course they will. Will the gains in that bank account be taxed? Sure it will. So now, let's review this average person that just five minutes ago looked like he was doing pretty well.

$3,000	Annual tax refund	0% rate of return	Tax-free
$150,000	401(k)	6% rate of return	Taxable
$100,000	Equity in home	0% rate of return	Tax-free
$20,000	Investment fund	6% rate of return	Taxable
$10,000	Bank savings	1.5% rate of return	Taxable

Once again, take a step back and look at how this person is doing financially. Not only are the return rates not glamorous, but when there is a rate of return, there is a tax on those gains. Remember, this is a typical scenario.

I would like to stop and say that we are finished with this person, but another situation needs to be discussed. Are there fees and charges attached to these assets? Unfortunately, the answer is yes. Is there a fee for the tax refund? Well, you may have had to hire an accountant to help you get your money back, and I would consider that a fee, so the answer is yes. Are there fees and management and expense charges in the 401(k)? Absolutely. Are there fees and service charges attached to your mortgage that includes the equity in your home? The answer is yes. In a typical investment fund, are there fees, management and trade charges? Yes. Are there fees in the bank accounts? Absolutely. So, let's summarize this one last time.

$3,000	Tax refund	0% return	Tax-free	Fees
$150,000	401(k)	6% return	Taxable	Fees
$100,000	Equity in home	0% return	Tax-free	Fees
$20,000	Investment fund (IF)	6% return	Taxable	Fees
$10,000	Bank savings	1.5% return	Taxable	Fees

I'm sorry, but no matter how long I stare at this, it doesn't look very good. What do you see? The funny thing is, for each of these accounts, the average person hired an expert to help him get these results: an accountant for the refund, a pension consultant for the 401(k), a mortgage broker for the home, an investment broker for the investment funds, and that "bank specialist" for the bank savings account. One way or another, this average person is paying these so-called experts. He has hired five experts, and none of them knows what the other one is doing. There is no plan and no coordination. The combined result of all this expert advice is financially killing the average American.

It is time to take a fresh approach to this problem. It's time to change the traditional thought process that got everyone into this mess in the first place. Giving you more knowledge to help you make better financial decisions in the future is the answer. This could change your life forever. The amazing thing is that you can make these changes without spending one more dime than you are already spending.

Investing
and
Demographics

Investments

Two trains head toward each other on a single track, unaware of coming events. Yet miles apart, everything on each train seems normal, just another day. As they speed closer to each other, an onlooker from a distant hill begins to realize that a disaster is unfolding. Still, on the trains, everything is calm. But one must think that several decisions were made to put two trains heading toward each other on the same track. This just didn't happen by chance. By the time the trains see each other, blowing their whistles is not a solution; applying the brakes is not effective enough to reverse the collision course. Although impact is imminent and immediate, the actual cause of this sudden impact started long before its outcome.

We must be aware of certain elements that could change our investments and strategies in the near future. The warnings are out there. The problem is that they may not be recognized, as warnings and life will go on, just another day, while the certainty of a collision gets closer and closer. Your investments are headed straight for higher taxes, inflation, and spiraling costs, all caused by a dramatic and costly shift in demographics. There is also the threat of terror which could wreak havoc on our economy. Now is the time to think. Given more knowledge, you may have time to prepare, if and when these elements collide.

The problem is, what we have been told about investing may not be true. You must understand that some of the things we have been told about investing may be more opinion than fact. The one question you must ask, to clear up this matter of opinion vs. fact, is this: Is financial planning a science? The answer is NO. If it were a science, then no one would lose money. So, a lot of the information we receive is filled with more opinions and guesses than actual facts.

Take the media for instance. When it comes to finance, the media serves as more of a rearview mirror than a windshield. It is focused on what already happened rather than what is going to happen. By the time the media reports on something regarding finances, it is already too late to get involved. Many times, we end up shooting where the duck was, a little late and with little results. As an example, do you remember all the advertising from investment companies telling you to sell your stocks before the market fell in the late 1990s and even today? Now, you see it doesn't work that way. Even Harry Markowitz, the father of the Modern Portfolio Theory (the theoretical foundation for the current asset allocation craze), was quoted as saying in 1998 with respect to the way he invested his own retirement funds. "I should have completed the historical covariance of the asset classes and drawn an efficient frontier. Instead, I visualized my grief if the stock market went up and I wasn't in it, OR if it went way down and I was completely in it. My intention was to minimize my future regret. So, I split my contributions 50/50 between bonds and equities."[47] So much for the modern portfolio theory.

What are the everyday advisors saying? "How much money do you have? Where do you have it invested? How is it doing? Oh....we can do better than that! We can get you a better rate of return." But once again, every time I hear this, I must ask, who is the one at risk? You, or the person making the recommendation? The element of risk is not new in investing. As far back as 1916, a stock order receipt from Paine Webber stated in bold print, "This transaction was made at the curb and is done entirely at your risk." Almost 90 years later, nothing has changed. Today, as it was 90 years ago, many people have thoughts, but don't know how to think and that alone puts them at risk. Having knowledge and information financially are important allies.

Now, if someone could tell you what is going to happen in the next ten years, would you want that information? With this knowledge, you would be able to make better financial decisions in the future. Here are the changes that will impact your investments to the greatest extent in the next ten years:

---

[47] As quoted in "Five Investing Lessons from America's Top Pension Fund," by Jason Zweig, *Money*, January 1998.

- The aging population
- Fewer workers to maintain productivity
- The increasing cost of government social programs
- Increasing government debt
- Increasing taxation
- Our inability to save money
- Greater personal debt

All of these issues are real and are going to happen. All of these will change your approach when it comes to your investment strategies. You may discover you are on the same track heading towards serious problems. Will you be prepared?

Also, more money may be flowing out of the stock market than money going in. This will be caused by the tremendous shift of workers retiring. More money may be flowing out of the market via retirement incomes from 401(k)s than new money going into 401(k)s from new workers. The same is true for stocks. Older people seeking more secure investment returns will sell off the more risky stocks and seek more secure and fixed returns. But, if we have less workers in the workforce to buy these stocks, who will buy them? Let's face it: Anytime the stock market has more sellers than buyers, prices go down.

In a report to Congress, Alan Greenspan said that, due to demographic shifts, a significant increase in workers' productivity will be needed in order to maintain the value of stocks, as we now know them. In Greenspan's February 28, 2002, report to the Department of Labor, he addressed the issue of our aging population and its impact on our economy. He stated, in part, "This dramatic demographic change is certain to place enormous demands on our nation's resources. Demands we almost surely will be unable to meet unless action is taken. That action is better taken as soon as possible. The long-term budget outlook offers a vivid and sobering illustration. No one should expect productivity growth to be sufficient to bail us out. Stability would require an overall federal tax burden well above its long-term average. We will have no choice but to make significant structural adjustments in the major retirement programs. Tax-rate increases of sufficient dimensions to deal with our looming fiscal problems arguably pose significant risks to economic growth. The dimensions of the challenge are enormous. This situation will require difficult choices."[48]

Many of Greenspan's comments point to the demographic changes and the impact it will have on the economy, including investing. Not only will it change personal investing, but also the companies who rely on stock prices to help their research and development of the products they produce. These

---

[48] Remarks by Alan Greenspan, *Saving for Retirement*, at the 2002 National Summit of Retirement Savings, Department of Labor, Washington, D.C., February 28, 2002.

challenges will have a ripple effect on the entire overall economy. All of these issues could place a strain on future stock values. Having this information might help you prevent long-term future stock losses. It might encourage you to change your financial thought process in the future. You will be facing intense personal financial challenges in the very near future. Starting today, as you do every day, you are trying to achieve financial security, and at the end of our working careers, we want to strive for financial freedom. We have basically been told there is only one way to achieve your financial goals at retirement: by investing in stocks and mutual funds.

Between where you are today financially and where you ultimately end up at retirement lie many obstacles and unintended consequences. Between here and there, you will be experiencing greater transfers of your wealth than you can ever imagine. These transfers will occur sometimes unknowingly and unnecessarily. These transfers will happen. But between here and there, you will be confronted with other hazards that will impact your wealth. These hazards are the changing demographics, risks, misinformation, taxation, debt, and finally, but most of all, a lack of knowledge in applying financial lessons to your everyday life. Between now and your financial future, if you don't recognize these hazards, and continue to apply losing financial strategies, you will end up with a portfolio full of unintended consequences.

Unfortunately, the only solution we have been given to achieve our financial freedom is to invest in stocks and mutual funds, to diversify and create a balanced portfolio with a variety of different stocks. This idea of investing, as history goes, is fairly new. In 1980, 4.6 million families in the U.S. were involved in owning mutual funds. According to the U.S. census, over 54.2 million families are now invested in funds.[49] This reflects a tremendous explosion in investing. In 1989, 27.8% of an individual's financial assets were held in stocks. Today, that number has grown to 54%. Very creative marketing has led us to believe that investing in the market is the only way to achieve our financial goals. This created the never-ending search for higher rates of return. Competition to solicit your investment dollars is centered on that rate of return. Again, the one question I have is this: Whenever someone who wants your business says they can get you a higher rate of return, who is the one at risk? You, or the one making the recommendation?

If I told you that there was another way to increase your wealth without market risks and with very impressive results, would you want to pursue that type of planning? Understanding the efficiency of money and recognizing transfers of your wealth is critical because every time you try to increase your wealth, you may also increase transfers of your

---

[49] http://www.census.gov.

wealth. Greater taxation will be the biggest culprit. By trying to increase your wealth through investing in the market, you must also consider the elements that will impact your market returns. Remember, you are gambling that all of the following will not have an effect on your market returns: economic shifts, taxation, government regulation, interest rates, demographic shifts, global terror, media mania, fees, and expenses. The question is: How lucky do you feel? The remaining financial option you have is learning the efficiency of money. This is a simple yet effective method of uncovering transfers of your wealth that occurs unknowingly and unnecessarily in your daily life. If you learn to recapture these financial transfers, the returns will be staggering. Learning the efficiency of money creates no market risk; it creates liquidity, use, and control of your money; it eliminates and reduces transfers of your wealth, and creates many financial options and opportunities.

The competition for your investment dollars is the equivalent of a feeding frenzy. As a comparison, let's look at some choices you have. You could have your money in investment funds (IF). You might think you earned $6,000 from your investments, but you needed to risk $80,000 of your money to achieve that type of return. Your earnings would be reduced by taxes and also fees that were charged to you for maintaining and managing your account.

The banks also want to be in this business. They have created many of their own types of bank savings accounts (BS). These are typically known as Certificates of Deposit, or CDs. You could also earn $6,000 in one of these accounts, but you need over $180,000 in such an account to achieve this type of return. Oh, and yes, the gains are taxable, and yes, fees and penalties could apply.

Then, here comes the idea of internal savings (IS). You also can earn $6,000 a year by reducing the major transfers in your life, but the difference is you need NOTHING ($0.00) in an account to accomplish this. By the way, this $6,000 is tax free, and there are no fees or penalties attached to this. So, given a choice, do you want to plan your financial future on IF (Investment Funds), BS (Bank Savings), or something that IS (Internal Savings) going to happen.

When determining how to invest your money, you must consider the impact of taxation on your earnings. If you invested $5,000 a year in mutual funds and received an average of 10% rate of return and you were in a 31% tax bracket, in the sixteenth year, your annual tax on these investments would be greater than your $5,000 annual deposit. Typically, the taxes from these accounts are not paid out of the investment account, but usually are paid from your lifestyle money. It is a fact that every effort to improve yourself financially creates more transfers of wealth. The more you save, the greater amount of tax you must pay. What the public has been told about finances and investing leaves you with very little choice and creates the unintended consequences of paying more taxes and transferring away more of your wealth in the future. What you have been taught, and what investment people tell you to do, is part of the problem. You will end up paying more and more taxes as a result of their work. A better course of action would be to focus on helping you resolve the taxation problem that confronts you in the future, rather than compounding the problem.

The common approach to their solution is diversification of your assets, otherwise known as the balanced portfolio. A lot has been said about diversification and balancing investment portfolios. Balanced portfolios have a combination of risk and safety built in their design. Risk in stocks when the market is strong and safety in bonds when equities are not doing so well. In a normal fluctuating market, a balanced portfolio's goal is to be able to achieve a zero rate of return. When the equities are performing well, the bond returns will drag down your portfolio's average earnings. When bonds are performing well, your equities' values are probably falling. The result is close to, if not, zero percent. Remember, you also may be exposed to taxes even if you lose some of your money while investing. THEIR SOLUTION COULD BE SEEN AS PART OF THE PROBLEM!

The real solution to the investment problem is to attack the problem itself: TAXES. To win the financial game of life, you must design your portfolio to focus on the taxable event it will create. We know that qualified retirement plans will be taxed from dollar one when you start your withdrawals for retirement. Other investments you own may also be taxed on their growth annually. Creating a tax-free environment for your money at retirement could offset taxable income that will tremendously reduce the taxation problem. Remember, the demographic shifts are going to create enormous future tax problems for you and the government. Taxes are not going to go down. Understanding this is the key. By reducing the transfers, taxes being the largest transfer in your life, you will effectively create and retain more wealth than pursuing the risky challenge of chasing high rates of return in the market.

It is difficult to get to the right solutions when you start out with the wrong premise. Let's face it: The amount of financial knowledge being given to you is very limited. The content of that knowledge is often slanted toward solutions that will ultimately profit others more than it profits you. Understanding this will help you realize that your economic situation is a matter of choice, not chance. Giving you more knowledge will guide you in making different and better decisions.

Love Letters to Your Broker

Sometimes it is necessary to question traditional thinking. I can only imagine the responses you might receive from the following inquiries.

Dear Sir,

I purchased from you a number of mutual funds as part of my IRA (or other retirement accounts, 401(k), SEP, etc.). I am concerned that when I retire I will have to sell off these investments to provide income for myself. I am also concerned that, at the time I retire, many other boomers such as myself will also be selling off their stocks and mutual funds for income. Please provide me an analysis or estimate of the market supply and demand expectations when it's my time to retire.

If you can't provide me with data that reflects how huge amounts of stock and funds can be sold off by a greater number of people than there are buyers and still maintain the values I need to provide my retirement income, do you still advise me to buy more stocks and mutual funds for my retirement accounts? If so, why?

Please don't answer my question on the basis of historical market returns or how stocks compare with other investments. There has not been any published due diligence reports about how the full "stocks for retirement" cycle can work. Many published books say that retirement accounts have created an unintended consequence where trillions of dollars of mutual funds and stocks will have to be sold to a fewer number of buyers. Once again, do you still advise me to buy more stocks and mutual funds?

Sincerely,
Concerned Client

Dear Sir,

It has come to my attention that all of the money I have invested with you in my 401(k) and IRAs have guarantees attached to them. Insofar as I am guaranteed to lose 20% to 40% of my account due to taxation at retirement, is it still your recommendation to continue to fund these programs? On top of the guaranteed losses due to taxation, am I not exposed also to the everyday risks of the market? Regardless of market losses I incur, I am still guaranteed the tax losses at retirement.

Now, I have read a survey of average investors. The survey asked a few questions on the impact of terrorist attacks. Question one: What do you feel the odds are of another major terrorist attack occurring in the U.S. in the next five years? One hundred percent of the people responded that the odds were 100% that another attack would occur. Question two: If a terrorist attack does occur, do you feel it would affect our financial markets in a positive or negative way? One hundred percent of the people polled answered that the impact would be negative. Question three: How long do you believe this negative impact will last? One to three years? Three to five years? Five to ten years? Ninety percent of the people surveyed said three to five years.

Having all this information, is it still your recommendation to forgo these risks and to continue to fund these programs? If so, why?

Very truly yours,
Client

Dear Sir,

It has come to my attention that I may retire to a higher tax bracket than I'm in currently or than I was in when I first began working. The 401(k) and IRAs that I have been contributing to are not only exposed to the everyday market risks and risks of future higher taxation, but now also the risk of loss due to terrorist attacks.

I have also recently heard these comments regarding the economy that could also affect my investments:

"Ensuring fiscal stability would require an overall federal tax burden well above its long-term average . . ."

"We will eventually have no choice but to make significant structural adjustments in the major retirement programs. . ."

"Tax-rate increases of sufficient dimension to deal with our looming fiscal problems arguably pose significant risk to economic growth. . ."

"No one should expect productivity growth to be sufficient to bail us out. . ."

"We have already made promises to future generations that we will be unable to keep. . ."

These comments sounded like a scare tactic to me at first, until I found out that they came from Alan Greenspan in his report to the Department of Labor. Is it still your recommendation to continue to fund my qualified plans, even though I feel enormous risks in doing so? Do you have any studies or due diligence analyses of market conditions, taxation, and demographic conditions that will impact my retirement investments at the time I plan to retire? I would like to see that information.

Thanks,
Your Client

All of the points in these love letters should be a concern to you. These points are legitimate issues that involve your future and could dramatically change your life.

Retirement
Plans
and
Demographics

Qualified Plans

Qualified retirement plans remain a mystery even to those who blindly believe in their purpose. It is commonly understood that these plans will create great amounts of money for retirement and, at the same time, save taxes for everyone who participates in them. The government, CPAs, accountants, news media, financial planners, banks, investment brokers, benefit managers, and yes, even your parents will tell you that this is true. But the truth today is an elusive commodity. The truth is that a qualified plan (401(k), IRA, SEP, etc.) only does one thing. A qualified plan simply defers the taxes due to a later date, and possibly, just possibly, defers the taxes due to a higher tax table. Understanding the demographic shifts and the continuous over-spending of the government and its uncontrolled debt, it is logical to believe that taxes must go up in the future if our country is to survive.

If I could tell you the exact day that your retirement account will suffer its greatest loss, would you want to know that day? Then, in having that information, if you could do something now to prevent those losses, would you do it? You see, the day you retire and start receiving income from these accounts is the day your retirement accounts will suffer their greatest losses due to taxes.

As a bit of light humor, I ask younger workers who are involved in 401(k)s this simple question: "When you were filling out the paperwork for your 401(k), did you check the 30% or the 40% guaranteed loss box?" They give me a puzzled look. I tell them, "You see, when you retire, this account could be taxed 30% to 40% guaranteed, regardless of whether your account goes up or down in value."

Seriously though, the average 35-year-old worker who has been in the workforce for 10 to 12 years has experienced down or flat markets more than 50% of their working years. These people, in the future, will be confronted with record levels of taxation. For anyone planning to become successful in the future, the idea of deferring withdrawals of money to a later date only to have it taxed at a higher rate is crazy. If you are going to retire to a lower tax bracket, then, by all means, use a qualified plan to fund your retirement. You could realize an actual tax savings. The problem is, I believe, everyone's taxes will go up in the future, rich or poor.

Earlier, I gave reasons why qualified plans don't result in real tax savings. I also mentioned why the government is allowing you to put more and more money into these plans. The government understands very well the demographics shifts and how it will impact them. They simply need larger pools of money—your money—to tax in the future at whatever rate they can. Here again, the traditional thought is that the government is doing you a favor, when in reality they are preparing and protecting themselves.

There are some advantages to using qualified plans.

- Deposits are tax-deductible
- Creates a nest egg for retirement
- Earnings are tax-deferred
- Creates forced savings
- Your employer may match contributions
- Your plan may contain borrowing provisions

Along with the advantages, there are some disadvantages that you should also be aware of.

- Deferring taxes to a later date
- Future tax rates could increase
- Funds not available until age 59½ (with very few exceptions)
- Early withdrawal penalty
- Possible loss of Social Security benefits
- Deposits stop, if disabled
- Usually no death benefits
- Cannot use assets as collateral
- Total government control
- Administration expenses
- Possible penalties at 70½
- Loss of capital gains treatment
- Ever-changing laws

- Limited amounts into plan
- Funds possibly exposed to lawsuits
- Multi-state tax potential
- No deductions for losses in plan
- Limited beneficiary options
- Divorce causes tax problems
- Loan interest double taxed
- Possible losses in the market

How does that look? I must be honest though; I do have a qualified plan that I do set aside some money in. But I realized a while back that this should not be the only way to fund my retirement income. It's expensive, risky, and leaves me exposed to future taxation problems. Unfortunately, for many people, this is the only source for retirement income. Since 100% of this income is taxable, people end up becoming what I call "The Perfect Taxpayer." All of a taxpayer's income being taxable with no deductions makes a happy government. The question is: What will make you happy in a future that promises higher taxes and reduced benefits?

So far, as a reader of this book, you have a distinct advantage in preparing for the future. You now know certain events are going to happen that will impact everyone's financial future. If you KNOW something is going to happen, you can better prepare.

In the future, to survive financially, your focus should be centered on creating more tax-free elements into your retirement preparation. Remember, qualified plans only do two things. First, they defer taxes (what the public wants), and second, they defer tax calculations (what the government wants).

Owning a Home and Demographics

Owning a Home. . .
The Most Misunderstood
American Dream

Another victim of the changing demographics could be the housing industry. The idea that the value of homes will always increase is wrong. People today often miscalculate the increased values of their homes. They don't take into consideration the cost of maintenance, improvements, insurance, and taxes that are paid while they live there. The average homeowner may experience only a 2% or 3% growth rate of return, even though the value of his home may have increased by 40% in a ten-year period.

The numbers can be deceiving. As the general population gets older, many retirees may downsize and move to condos or retirement communities. After all, a 6,000-square-foot home requires a lot of maintenance and upkeep, not to mention the increasing cost and upward-spiraling property taxes. If the aging population sells their larger homes and builders continue to build larger homes at a record pace . . . who will buy them? The younger generation?

In 3,000 days, with two-thirds of the now-working population being 60 years old, or older, we will be dealing with a smaller number of new buyers. This young group of buyers will also want to build new homes for themselves. This will create an overabundance of larger homes in the marketplace. The rule of supply and demand may take over. Too much product and not enough buyers equal lower prices. The government and the banks will have to get more creative when it comes to buying a home. After all, this is a source of revenue for both of them. The banks want more buyers with bigger mortgages, and the government wants to keep the values of properties high, so it can tax those high values.

The starting point for most of the confusion and misinformation starts with how you pay for the home. You can pay cash or choose from a variety of mortgages from a bank or mortgage company. One important factor you must understand is this: Banks and mortgage companies want to collect the most amount of interest in the shortest period of time that they can. If they collected the exact same amount of interest in every type of mortgage in existence, there would only be one type of mortgage. Understand this, some mortgages will cost you more than others, and sometimes the truth of these costs is cleverly hidden by the lender. What appears to be true may not be true when it comes to the cost of your mortgage.

One thing is for certain though: Whether you pay cash or get a mortgage to pay for your home, you will suffer a transfer of your wealth. If you finance your home with a mortgage, you must pay interest on that loan until it is paid off. If you pay cash for your home, then you lose the interest you could have earned on that money. This is known as a lost opportunity cost. What is a lost opportunity cost? Well, if you spend a dollar, not only do you lose that dollar, but you also lose the ability to earn money from that dollar. You will have to make lost opportunity cost a serious consideration when trying to determining how to pay for your home.

A glaring example of lost opportunity cost is its impact on the down payment of your home. If you put $30,000 down on your new home, not only do you lose your $30,000, but also the money you could have earned from it. If you could have earned 7% on this $30,000, it would have earned another $30,290 in ten years, or $91,162 in twenty years, or $182,324 in thirty years. When discussing your options with the mortgage company, all that you would be told is that the more money you put down on your new home, the smaller the monthly payment will be. But, if you are considering paying cash for your home, or putting a sizeable amount towards a down payment, we must first ask this question: As an investment, is this a good investment and a good place to keep your money?

If you bought a home ten years ago for $125,000 and now the value of your home is $200,000, that seems like an enormous increase, but let's do the math. The $75,000 increase over a 10-year period gives you a 4.81% rate of return on the value of your house. But, let's look deeper at what drove the value of your home skyward. Did you make any improvements to your home over that 10-year period? These improvements would include general maintenance, remodeling, a new furnace, new carpeting, a new roof, landscaping improvements—the list goes on and on. Let's say that during the 10 years you lived there, you made $15,000 in improvements. These improvements helped drive the value of your home from $125,000 to $200,000. If we include the cost of improvements into the equation, the rate of return on your home is now 3.63%.

If we are considering the home as an investment, there is one more element that you must consider: Taxes. We must agree on one thing. Property values continue to be assessed at higher rates by state and local governments, and the tax rates on property could and will increase. With your house being considered as an investment, let's look at its after-tax rate of return. Let's say you paid an average of $3,000 per year in property taxes. Over a 10-year period, that would be $30,000. Now, with taxes and improvements included, that $75,000 increase in the $125,000 home in a 10-year period comes to a 1.64% after-tax rate of return on your home. How does that now compare with other investments that were available to you over the past 10 years?

Everyone is excited about property values going up, I mean everyone. First of all, you're excited because you feel you have made a wise financial decision. But, don't go feeling too special, because all the houses around you have increased in value at about the same pace. The banks are also excited about housing prices. Mortgaging more expensive homes means more interest for them. Also, as property values rise, so does the use of equity loans, which in turn increases the amount of interest banks collect.

State and local governments are also very excited about property values going up. Depending on the state you're living in, property values could be assessed as frequently as every year. It would be hard to imagine assessed values on property ever going down. You see, the state government's assessment increases means more money for the state in the form of property-tax revenues. Local and city governments use these assessments as the basis for school taxes. For personal reasons, the government wants to make sure values continue to increase.

It wasn't too long ago that both the banks and the government realized that it was in their best interests to keep the values of these properties as high as they could. The banks, with the urging of the Federal Government, became creative with the types of mortgages offered. These new mortgages help more people qualify for more expensive homes (more interest for them, more taxes for the government). The Federal Government recently introduced their acceptance of 40-year mortgages and also reverse mortgages (for people over 62 years of age). These 40-year mortgages would help to keep property values high. With longer durations to pay, people could afford more expensive homes (more taxes for the government, more interest for the bank).

My point is that the increases in some of these property values are driven by the greed of the banks and the government. It is also my opinion that if property values do go down, interest rates and property taxes won't. As a result, the equity in your home will decrease dramatically. When selling your home, the property taxes and the interest rates are not negotiable. Only the equity in your home is. A buyer for your home evaluates if they can afford the property taxes, the bank's interest rates, and your asking price. If a number has to be lowered in the selling transaction, it is your asking price that will be reduced, not the taxes or the interest rates. So, the only one at risk here is the homeowner.

Once again, with this information, do you feel that this home or your home is a great investment and a good place to put as much money as you can? Not only must you understand the rate of return on the value of your home, but also if your home is an investment, we have to take into consideration the rate of return on the down payment, and also the rate of return on the equity that you have built up in your home. If you think that there is some complicated equation to calculate these answers, there isn't. The answer is always the same . . . zero!

The bank or mortgage company is not sending you a monthly dividend check on the money you gave them as a down payment on your home. Not only that, but your down payment is not accessible to you even through a loan because it is not part of the mortgage. So, on your down payment, you will continue to receive 0% return forever. Good deal, huh? This zero percent rate of return also applies to the equity in your home. Again, no calculation is needed. You see, your equity doesn't drive the value of your property up. Your property values will go up whether you have $100,000 of equity in your home, or only $1 of equity in it. But you may have been told that having a lot of equity in your home and keeping it there is a good thing.

What if property values go down? Would this be a good place to keep your money at a 0% rate of return? If the housing market went down, would you rather have $100,000 of equity in your home, or $1 of equity? PLEASE NOTE: I AM NOT CONDONING, SUPPORTING, OR EVEN SUGGESTING TAKING YOUR EQUITY OUT OF YOUR HOME AND INVESTING IT IN THE STOCK MARKET. I am saying that you should have access, liquidity, use, and control of that money. It can become a very powerful financial tool for you. What makes this a valuable tool is that the equity in your home is also tax-FREE money (subject to IRS limitations). But, there are a number of issues that could impact this tax-free money (equity) and drive the value of your home down.

There are a growing number of practitioners in the financial services industry who feel you should strip the equity out of your home. This thought process is planted firmly in the idea that property values will always rise. Most of us know that this is not true. What must be measured and calculated is what really constitutes a true increase in property values, as opposed to inflation-adjusted property values, and also whether increases in personal incomes are keeping pace. From a percentage standpoint, if yearly property taxes continue to outpace the growth (or lack thereof) of personal incomes, then utilizing all the equity in your home could create greater unintended con-sequences. Remember, creating new debt to finance another investment is subject not only to the repayment of that debt, but also pressures from inflation, ever-increasing taxes, and the constantly changing housing industry. Demographic changes will also have an impact on this scenario. To my knowledge, no one has been able to predict inflation rates accurately, nor predict increases in property taxes, future interest rates, nor the fluctuations in the housing industry. Unfortunately, some people think they can. Even worse, when they are trying to convince you to take all the equity out of your home, they ignore these possible future compli-cations completely. Let yourself dream for a second. You refinanced your home to the max to get your equity, and two months later, a pedophile moves in next door to you. What just happened to the value of your home? Is that a good dream or a bad dream?

All things considered, you may want to rethink your equity and mortgage situation. You may be exposed to bad neighbors, shifting housing markets, future demographics, shifts in population, changing neighborhoods, taxation, and higher interest rates. Let's first start with interest rates. As we all know, interest rates fluctuate all the time, but how can it impact your equity and value of your home? Well, in buying a house, a purchaser is always qualified on the amount that he or she can afford to pay on a monthly basis. So, when interest rates are low, less monthly money would go toward interest payments and more toward the principal of the house. If a buyer qualified for an $850 monthly payment, with a 5.5% 30-year mortgage, he could purchase a $150,000 home. But, if mortgage interest rates rose to 8%, that buyer can now only afford a $116,000 house that carries an $851 monthly mortgage payment. You may have to lower the price of your home to attract buyers in the right price range.

Can interest rates go up? Sure they can. They have in the past. Remember the Jimmy Carter era? Interest rates were 12%, 15%, 18%. Housing prices and values fell. What little gains there were in housing values, if any, were eaten up by inflation. Something just as scary as higher interest rates is just over the horizon. Be aware of the changing demographics. With a record number of new houses being built, fewer number of younger buyers, the older population downsizing their larger homes, a greater number of debt-plagued buyers entering the market, and ever-increasing property taxes and maintenance costs, the housing real estate market may become flooded.

Once again, this may create a problem with supply and demand. Too many homes for sale and not enough qualified buyers means prices will fall. Along with the resale value declining, so will your tax-free equity in your home. The stunning shift in the demographics in the next 3,000 days is going to happen. Should you be investing in, and keeping as much money in your home as you can? Be careful of your answer.

Still another situation that can create a loss of value in your home is bad neighbors. You're sitting in your home looking out the window at the new landscaping project you just completed. There's a knock at your front door. There, standing on your porch, is a guy you have never seen before. You crack the door open, and he says, "Howdy! My name is Bubba. I'm your new neighbor. I've got six dogs; they're all pretty friendly except for that one with no hair . . . if I were you, I wouldn't try to pet him. I've got four kids. Aren't kids a hoot? I'll tell you, between parole officers and social workers, kids sure keep you busy. My wife, now there's a fine woman. You might see her from time to time. She's gonna re-upholster furniture right out there on the front porch to make extra money. Me, well, I'm a work-at-home kinda guy. I'll be rebuilding truck engines right here in the driveway. If you ever need my help, just let me know. See you later, buddy!" This is more like: See you later, property values.

That example may seem a little extreme, but a neighbor like that would dramatically impact the value of your home and the tax-free equity in your home. Even a neighbor who didn't maintain their property very well would affect your home's value and your ability to sell it at market prices. So, when deciding what type of mortgage you should have, the size of your down payment, or even if you are thinking paying cash for a home, be sure to consider the housing market, demographics, neighbors, and shifting interest rates. Paying off your house may be more beneficial to the bank or mortgage company than it is to you.

Now that we've discussed your home as an investment and whether or not it's a good place to keep tax-free money, let's talk about someone who may still be interested in paying cash for their home. I know that buying a home is an emotional decision. Let's try to put some of the emotions aside by using simple math. Usually, you are told that by paying cash for your house, you would save all that interest you would have normally paid inside a mortgage. On the surface, that is correct. After all, a $150,000 home with a 30-year mortgage at 7% interest would create $359,262 in payments. One could come to the conclusion that by paying

$150,000 in cash for the house, you saved $209,262 in interest payments. But, if that same $150,000 you paid in cash earned 7% for 30 years, you would have earned $1,217,474. The difference between the $359,262 you would have paid, if you had a mortgage, and the $1,217,474 you could have saved is huge.

Let me ask you one question: Do you believe that you will be able to sell that $150,000 house for $1,217,474 in 30 years? The difference between saving $209,262 in interest and not being able to earn $1,217,474 is called the spread. The spread in this case is $1,008,212. That is a huge lost opportunity cost. The cost of losing $1,217,474 over a 30-year period is equal to a lost opportunity cost of $3,381 per month. From a different perspective, it costs $3,381 per month to live in your "paid cash for" home. Remember, a down payment of $30,000 in this scenario also creates a lost opportunity cost. A $30,000 down payment at 7.2% would have created more money than the actual total cost of the home when you purchased it.

In all the lessons we are discussing, the focus is on maintaining liquidity, use, and control of your money. It is also just as important to reduce or eliminate as many lost opportunity costs as possible. Continuing to think a layer deeper about how you are purchasing your home, you must also consider the impact of inflation. Failing to consider the forces of inflation on your money could be costly. Let's take a look.

109

With an inflation rate averaging 2.5%, you must understand the buying power of your dollar in the future. A thousand dollars today will only have the buying power of $781 in 10 years. In 20 years, that buying power will be reduced to $610, and to only $476 in 30 years. Knowing this, I have to ask you a question: If given a choice, would you want to make more payments on your house now, when your buying power is high, or make the same payment much later when your dollar power has been discounted by inflation? If I can buy the same house with discounted dollars, then that is what I want to do.

I bring out the point of inflation to demonstrate and compare longer mortgages to shorter ones. The bank will tell you that you will save on interest by selecting the shorter mortgage. They say it will reduce the overall cost of the loan. What the banks are really saying is, "We want to charge you as much interest as we can while getting the money we lent you back as fast as we can." This game was invented by the banks to create velocity of money for them. This program profits the banks more than it profits you. Remember, the only ways a bank makes money is by charging interest and fees. Why would they want to reduce their profits by urging you not to pay interest? It doesn't make sense until you understand exactly what they are doing.

Let's compare a couple of mortgages to see which one would be more profitable for you. Take a look at a 15-year and a 30-year mortgage of

$150,000. At 6.5%, a 15-year mortgage would have a $1,307 monthly payment. A 30-year mortgage at 7% would have a payment of $998 per month. There is a $309 difference in the monthly payments on these mortgages. If you were able to save $309 per month for 30 years at 8%, you would have $463,591.

Someone might argue that after paying off your 15-year mortgage, you could save $1,307 per month at 8% for 15 years while the other person is still paying off his 30-year mortgage. A savings of $1,307 per month at 8% for 15 years would earn $455,287. The 30-year mortgage comes out on top. You should also know this: If you could save $309 per month by using a 30-year mortgage, what rate of return would you need on $309 a month to be able to pay off your house in the 15th year? Just a 5.69% after-tax rate of return. Maintaining liquidity, use, and control of your money is key to financial success and can create more opportunities for you.

Another factor to consider is that there are more tax deductions in the first 15 years of a 30-year mortgage than there are in the entire 15-year mortgage. Your tax-deductible savings in your home mortgage should also be a consideration in helping you select the right mortgage. In a 31% tax bracket, a $150,000 mortgage at 6.5% for 15 years creates a $26,412 tax savings. A 30-year mortgage for the same house at 7% yields a $64,872 tax break.

If interest rates increase, don't be alarmed if the selling value of your house falls. We have warned you that you may have to lower the price to sell it due to higher interest rates. Paying your house off as fast as you can when rates are low could cost you dearly. If interest rates increase, maintaining liquidity, use, and control of your money is vital. In a home that is supported by two incomes, what happens if an income earner becomes disabled? Can you then go to the bank and try to get some of your tax-free equity out of your house to help your family get through a difficult period? You can try, but you won't get it. With the loss of a breadwinner, the bank will conclude that you have no way to pay that loan back. Consider this: 48% of all home foreclosures are due to someone becoming disabled.

Now that you have received some information and gained some knowledge about owning and purchasing a home, once again, the question is: Is your home a good place to safely keep a lot of your money? In light of possible foreclosures and the bubble bursting in the housing industry, the equity in your home could be at risk. You know the old saying about real estate that it's all about location, location, location? Well, with the shift in demographics and a housing crisis, you'd better learn the phrase, it's all about timing, timing, timing.

With all the uncertainty in the world today financially, politically, and otherwise, we are all seeking safe harbors in our lives. The only way to create this is to gain more wisdom and knowledge. Having personal control of your finances is the key in surviving the coming historical changes. The answer is not to follow the traditional thinking of the past. You may discover that the people giving you advice have profited from your money than you did. These financial transfers to others are robbing you of your wealth.

There Are Solutions

First, understand the real value of your home. Don't get excited when you see the value of your home going up. Do the math. That increase in the value of your home may also cost you more in property taxes and insurance. Second, eliminate as many transfers of your wealth as you can. Choose the right mortgage for you, not the bank. Do the math. What seems to be true on the surface may not be true in the long run. Also, never pay cash for your home unless you are filthy rich and don't care. You need to understand liquidity, use, and control of your money, as well as lost opportunity cost. It will change your life and the way you think about money. Next, establish an equity line of credit and learn to use it as a financial tool. This equity line of credit can help you establish your own personal bank which will aid you in the future. Learn to finance your cars, help fund college tuition, prepare for retirement, and reduce debt, with the possibility of deducting these interest payments from your taxes. Finally, find a trusted advisor who is educated in identifying and eliminating wealth transfers in your life. Your goals should start with learning more and knowing more. That is the solution.

The
Changing
Demographics
The
Next
3,000
Days

Washington Is Broken

Our government and the results of their lack of leadership and planning over the last 40 years have assured that our near and distant future is guaranteed to collide with reality. America, and its people, has never lost its greatness but we have been sold down the river by leadership filled with greed, corruption, lies, and a lack of courage and respect. The social fabric of our country is unwinding. I am afraid that the moral and ethical decay thrust upon us by our elected officials is a sign of dramatic changes. Ideology and social engineering have put our country on the verge of collapse. Fiscal irresponsibility and decision making by our leaders have led us to the brink of financial failure.

With the fall of the investment banks, the Fannie and Freddie collapses, and credit and solvency crunches, the next 3,000 days for America surviving as a nation will be critical. In the next several years, America is facing several threats that could destroy its social foundation.

The Loss of the Family

The family was once the center point for American life. The family supplied the morals, ethics, and values that made us a great nation. The decline of family values signaled the decline of common sense and personal responsibility.

The Size of Government

In the last 50 years, the size of the government has grown three and a half times faster than the economy. The size of the government alone robs its citizens of their ability to save for their future. The government has been ruling with only a 10% to 20% approval rating by its people. Government arrogance is suffocating.

Media Manipulation

We no longer receive the news; it is editorialized and "opinionized" to meet the agendas of the news organizations. The news media is more suspect of creating headlines than reporting the news. The media is big business and needs to make money no matter what. It can be very dangerous when the media's agenda can destroy people, their lives, and our country.

Educational Productivity

We are falling behind in the world of education. The level of our decline goes unnoticed and unreported. The government approach is to simply throw more taxpayers dollars at a broken system. In the last 20 years, it seems that the educational institutions have also formed an agenda. History does not have to be re-written, and the philosophy that America is the problem must be dealt with. Teach our kids to compete and inspire them to succeed.

Energy Dependency

America has the ability and resources to become the energy leaders of the world, but ignorance keeps getting in our way. The agenda of leadership and a do-nothing attitude leaves us enslaved to a pathetic cause. We feed the hatred of America because our government forces us to do so by supporting dictatorial nations where we must buy our energy. We are held hostage by stupidity. Energy impacts our economy, our standard of living, our national security, and our freedom.

America's Debt Dependency

During the Cold War, we spent Russia out of existence. Our politicians are now doing the same to us. Over 10 trillion dollars of government debt and increasing government programs are turning us into a socialized society that over time will destroy us a nation.

International Debt

Piece by piece, bit by bit, we are selling our nation to other countries. Foreign nations will have the power to determine our future and influence our course of action. This is very dangerous to our country's survival.

Individually, each of these elements could cause havoc in a society, but the thought of dealing with all or most of these concerns is overwhelming. Each one of these problems has something in common: government involvement. So, it is with a pound of fear and an ounce of disbelief when they get involved in our economic solutions. All too often, their solution to the problem is to have us, the taxpayers, pay for their mistakes, and they have a history of mistakes.

What Is and Is About to Be

Inside your mind and your thoughts only you can measure the extent of our country's problems. Hopefully, you are not of the simplistic solution that the government will solve everything. Personal responsibility is a funny phrase. Another way to view it is your ability to respond. If you have the ability to know and understand what is going to happen in the near future, that is truly a gift. With that information, you can respond in a way that can help you. If you could respond to events and were able to improve your financial situation, you would want to know it now.

The Changing Demographics

Let's imagine we could pile all of your wealth in the middle of a table. All the wealth you have, and even your ability to earn more money, is stacked up on this table. No matter how much money you have, you want your money to grow.

Traditional planning tells us that, to make your wealth grow, you must invest in the right stocks and mutual funds. To increase your wealth, you must simply select the investments that will get you a higher rate of return. When attempting to achieve higher rates of return, who is the one at risk—you or the people making investment recommendations? This is what we call a product solution. All you have to do is to buy the right investments at the right time and then sell them when they reach their highest value before everyone else does. The product solution has been the center point of traditional planning.

The problem is, it is difficult to get to the right solution when you start out with the wrong premise. Einstein once said, "You can't solve a problem using the same thought process that created the problem in the first place." The real challenge, financially, isn't what product will increase your wealth, but the underlying elements that will decrease its value. The real issue that will compound and accelerate our government's financial demise and destroy personal financial freedom in the future is the dramatically changing demographics. This is an event that we are certain is going to happen, and it will have dramatic financial consequences.

Men in Black

David Walker wore many hats as the Comptroller General of the United States, including head of the General Accountability Office (GAO), lead partner on the audit of the U.S. Government's consolidated financial statements, and the de facto chief accountability officer of the Federal Government. He now travels the nation warning of an impending crisis. "I am desperately trying to get people to understand the significance of this for our country, our children, and our grandchildren. How this is resolved could affect not only our economic security but our national security.[50]

"We are headed toward a future where we will have to double federal taxes or cut federal spending by 60%."[51] But the documentation of this problem has not prompted political action to address this. Future government obligations for Medicare and Social Security alone are 10 times the size of the national debt. The problem is, if any politician dares to even mention cutting Social

---

[50] "The looming national benefit crisis," by Dennis Cauchon and John Waggoner, *USA Today*, October 3, 2004.
[51] *Id.*

Security, he will get voted out of office. All of this was mentioned in a *USA Today* front-page article on October 3, 2004. It also reported that in Alan Greenspan's report to the Department of Labor, he stated, "As a nation, we have already made promises to coming generations of retirees that we will be unable to fulfill."[52] You see, if you know what is going to happen in the next 3,000 days, you will have a clearer view to make better financial decisions.

It's Not What You Know, It's When You Know It

If prior to 9-11, I would have predicted that you would wake up every day to color-coded terror alerts, that the Twin Towers in New York would be attacked and destroyed, that thousands of Americans would die on American soil, that we would be involved in a war, that the stock market would suffer tremendous losses, that the airline industry would be near collapse, that major scandals would rock Enron, WorldCom, Arthur Andersen, Kmart, and many others . . . would you have believed me? If you had this information, you would have had the opportunity to prepare for these events in advance.

---

[52] *Id.*

Facing the Future

In the next 3,000 days, we know certain demographic shifts are going to occur that will impact your financial future dramatically. Here is a partial list of events that will change your life:

• **Fewer Tax-paying Workers**. From a percentage standpoint, there will be a larger growing number of retirees on government programs than the number of actual tax-paying workers. Alan Greenspan commented that we won't have the workforce or the productivity to feed, clothe, or house the larger retired population.[53]

• **More Retirees on More Government Programs, Living Longer**. This is happening as you read this book. In 3,000 days, there is going to be a tremendous increase in the number of people living on government programs (Medicare, Medicaid, Social Security, etc.). These people will surpass the life expectancies the government estimated 20 years ago. The cost of these programs increases every year regardless of the number of participants. The government's own 2000 Census confirms that these events are going to continue to happen at a

---

[53] Remarks by Alan Greenspan, *Saving for Retirement*, at the 2002 National Summit of Retirement Savings, Department of Labor, Washington, D.C., February 28, 2002.

tremendous cost to a workforce with less taxpaying workers.[54]

• **More Money Flowing Out of 401(k)s than Money Flowing In**. For the first time in the history of government-qualified retirement plans (401(k)s, IRAs, SEPs, etc.), more money could be flowing out of these programs for retirement income than new money flowing in to these plans via new worker contributions. This is a dilemma. If an ever-growing retirement population is cashing in their retirement funds, will the smaller workforce be able to buy up all of these investments? We may run into the problem of too many retirees selling off funds and not enough new workers to buy them.

• **Increasing Government Debt (Not Deficit)**. In the last 50 years, on a year-to-year basis, the debt of the Federal Government has never gone down. Not once! The government continues to spend $1.35 for every dollar they collect in tax revenues. Politicians continue to look the other way, as our nation's debt explodes. While the government deficit is the amount of overspending by the government on an annual basis, the government debit is the total accumulation of all its past debts. The government is paying over $350 billion annually just on the interest for this debt. The government is deeply concerned about interest rates on this debt going up, rightfully so.

---

[54] http://www.census.gov.

• **Seniors Selling Off Stocks for More Conservative (Less Risk) Returns**. In Greenspan's report to the Department of Labor, he stated that as people retire, they have a natural tendency to select more conservative, less risky investments. Once again, this may mean more people selling off stocks and mutual funds to purchase Certificates of Deposit (CDs) and fixed accounts. Between withdrawing money from 401(k) and pension accounts for retirement income, and the selling off of stocks and mutual funds for less risky outcomes, the question remains: Who will buy all these investments being sold? When there are more sellers than buyers for these products, will prices go down? Supply and demand will always determine prices.

• **More Seniors Downsizing Their Homes**. With the ever-increasing maintenance costs, insurance premiums, and property taxes on large homes, it would not be unrealistic for elderly people to sell off these five and six thousand-square foot homes for something they can manage and afford. Home builders continue to build a record number of large homes aimed at a smaller proportion of buyers who can afford large homes. Of course, if too many homes are on the market at one time, prices would have to be adjusted downward in order just to sell them.

• **Effects of Record Amounts of Personal Debt**. Last year alone, there was credit expansion in the United States of $2,718 billion, combined with a zero increase in personal savings. You cannot borrow your way to prosperity. A new worker, right out of college, is entering the workforce with about $40,000 of college debt and an unbalanced checkbook, and these are the smart ones. Record numbers of single-parent households offer very little room for financial success. Personal debt slows the buying ability of an economy and the ability to save money for the future (purchasing stocks and mutual funds). The overall debt and total liabilities of the United States Government is $52 trillion. That is three times more money than is currently printed in the whole world today.

• **Increasing Taxation—Decreasing Benefits**. Get ready because these two elements are going to happen. No one should be surprised, but, of course, they will be. Members of the government are not denying that this is going to happen. They just haven't figured out yet how and when to say so and still get elected. The game will always be to blame the other guy, but that game solves nothing.

• **Market Uncertainty (Risks, Future Taxation, Terror)**. One thing for sure that is going to happen, as it has and always will, is uncertainty in the investment markets. From an investor's standpoint, the stock market goes up and down, as it has and always will. That hundred-page prospectus that you're supposed to read when you buy an investment product should have an airsickness bag attached to it. If the market were a ride at Disney World, you would wait for hours in line to get on it. Up and down and round and round it goes, and you have no control over it. As Greenspan eluded, we may not have the workforce or the productivity to maintain the values of stocks as we now know them. Issues of more money flowing out of 401(k) accounts than is flowing in and seniors selling off more risky investments for more conservative ones also come into play.

The government, in its search for more revenue, may find that increasing taxes on investments is a way of sustaining its addictive habit of overspending their revenues and budgets and increasing the burden of debt on society. They are already calculating how to tax the unborn to pay for and support the undead. And now there is terror. Someone nine thousand miles away is trying to figure out how to destroy our financial infrastructure through terror. Little do they know that we are succeeding at inflicting the same result on ourselves.

I have now discussed with you ten events that are certain to impact your financial future. The problem is this: THESE ISSUES CANNOT BE SOLVED BY BUYING MORE STOCKS! You have to prepare for this future differently than the conventional wisdom that is out there today.

Boo!

We are living in a very historic time, and changes will have to be made. To some, this will sound scary. You see, I could consult you in fear, or I could consult you in truth, but, in today's world, fear and truth almost sound the same. But what we believe to be true could be part of the problem. For example, if I were to say. . .

- We face demands we almost surely will be unable to meet, unless action is taken.
- That action is better taken as soon as possible.
- Long-term budget outlook offers a vivid and sobering illustration of the challenges.
- No one should expect productivity growth to be sufficient to bail us out.
- Ensuring fiscal stability would require an overall federal tax burden well above its long-term average.
- We will eventually have no choice but to make significant structural adjustments in the major retirement programs.
- Tax-rate increases of sufficient dimensions to deal with our looming fiscal problems arguably pose significant risks to economic growth.

- The dimensions of the challenge are enormous.
- This situation will require difficult choices.[55]

You might come to the conclusion that I was simply trying to scare you. The reality, though, is that these are statements made by Alan Greenspan in his February 28, 2002, testimony to the Department of Labor. Now that's scary.

What's in Store

The demographic changes will impact every aspect of your financial life. Having the knowledge to deal with these changes is the real center point of your financial future and growth. The shifting demographics will impact qualified retirement plans, owning a home, your investments, and your retirement dramatically. To make things worse, the demographic changes will affect the way the government does business with us. It will impact taxation, future government programs, the cost of living, and the overall government debt. No investment product will solve these problems.

The demographic challenges will create even greater transfers of your wealth in your everyday life. Understanding this will give you a defining

---

[55] Remarks by Alan Greenspan, *Saving for Retirement*, at the 2002 National Summit of Retirement Savings, Department of Labor, Washington, D.C., February 28, 2002.

moment in the way you think about money. That defining moment comes with understanding the efficiency of money. This is a simple yet effective method of uncovering and reducing transfers of your wealth that occur every day unknowingly and unnecessarily.

If Something You Thought to Be True, Wasn't True. . .

Let's look at an example. Everyone believes, and is told to believe, that qualified plans, such as IRAs or 401(k)s, are tax-saving vehicles. If people 45 years of age were to deposit $2,000 into an IRA and they were in a 25% tax bracket, what would that tax savings be for doing this?

Well, 25% of $2,000 is $500, which is thought to be the tax savings. If they could earn 10% on this money, the $2,000 deposit would double every 7.2 years. At age 66, they would have $16,000 in their IRA account, and if they had invested and earned 10% on their tax savings of $500, it would have grown to $4,000 at age 66.

Unfortunately, the $500 "tax savings" was subject to capital gains tax over those years and they would have paid another $480 in taxes, leaving them with $3,520 in that account. Now, when they go to withdraw that $16,000 from the IRA at age 66, they would owe taxes on it. If they are lucky enough to still be in a 25% tax bracket when they retire, they owe $4,000 in taxes on the $16,000, but they only have $3,520 from their so-called tax savings to pay it. If you understand the impact of the demographics, do you believe taxes in the future are going to go up or down? Is it possible that you may retire to a higher tax bracket, let's say 35%? If that were the case, you owe the government $5,600 on your $16,000 withdrawal, but still only have $3,520 in savings to pay for it. You have to remember one important question: Whose future are you financing—yours or the Federal Government's?

Every Day Is a Tax Day

There is one thing a politician is fearful of: not getting elected. When it comes to taxes, they try to stay away from the topics of the federal income tax and the social security tax. These are hot buttons for voters. In the last couple of elections, these taxes have not increased because these taxes make headlines. But every year nets the government another record harvest of tax revenues—which they quickly outspend. How do they continue to collect record amounts of revenue every year, one might ask. Other than the income tax and social security tax, very quietly, just about all other taxes that don't make headlines have gone up 20% to 30% over the last five years. I call these taxes 'hidden taxes.' These silent killers are robbing us of our ability to save, which, by the way, is also taxed.

Taxes

Federal Income Tax ■ Social Security Tax ■ State
Tax ■ City Tax ■ County Tax ■ Property Tax ■
School Tax ■ Sales Tax ■ Estate Tax ■ Gasoline
Tax ■ Water Tax ■ Sewer Tax ■ Business Tax ■
Airport Tax ■ Telephone Tax ■ License Tax ■
Hotel Tax ■ Cable TV Tax ■ User Taxes ■
Unemployment Tax ■ Cigarette Tax ■ Corporate
Income Tax ■ Inheritance Tax ■ Accounts
Receivable Tax ■ Inventory Tax ■ Marriage
License Tax ■ Liquor Tax ■ Building Permit Tax
■ Medicare Tax ■ Fishing License Tax ■ Real
Estate Tax ■ Food License Tax ■ Fuel Permit
Tax ■ Hunting License Tax ■ Road Usage Tax
(truckers) ■ Luxury Tax ■ Recreational Vehicle
Tax ■ Utility Tax ■ Septic Permit Tax ■ Well
Permit Tax ■ Road Toll Booth Tax ■ Vehicle
Sales Tax ■ Workers' Compensation Tax ■
Trailer Registration Tax ■ Watercraft
Registration Tax ■ Long-term Capital Gains Tax
■ Short-term Capital Gains Tax ■ Telephone
Federal Excise Tax ■ Telephone State and Local
Tax ■ Telephone Usage Charge Tax ■ Telephone
Federal Universal Service Fee Tax ■ Telephone
Recurring Charges Tax ■ Tax on Energy, Gas,
Electric, Heating Oil

The ability to survive the trauma of the
taxation issue is compounded by the government's
enormous amount of debt. The interest on this debt

alone eats up a tremendous amount of the revenue the government collects from us via taxes. As the debt continues to soar, so does the interest. Along with their spending increases, the government is going to have to insist on collecting more revenue (higher taxes) to pay for what they are doing.

Only one division of the government must tell the truth about government debt. The President? No. The Congress? No. The Treasury? No. The GAO? No. There is only one department that must tell the truth. It is the Bureau of Public Debt. This is where foreign countries go to decide whether to invest in our T-bills and government bonds. The bureau has its own web site and lists the debt daily.[56] Remember, in the last 50 years, there has never been a year when this debt went down. This will have a tremendous impact on future taxes and your money.

Tax-a-Rama

Taxes are the greatest transfers of your wealth. If you believe that taxes are going to go down in the near future, then I'm truly concerned about you. Recent tax history and the government's spending habits are leading us in only one direction: higher taxes.

---

[56] http://www.treasurydirect.gov/NP/BPDLogin?application=np.

Tax Facts

- In recent years, personal taxes increased 42% faster than personal incomes.
- State and local government taxes increased 168% faster than national income.
- The typical American pays more in taxes than on food, shelter, and clothing combined.
- Federal taxes increased 2.5 times faster than personal income from 1995–2007, with more planned.
- 5.1 months equates to about 40% (142.5 days) of the year worked by the average citizen to pay for government spending at all levels.
- The average worker needed to work 1.4 months in 1928 to pay for federal plus state/local government spending, compared to working 5 months today. That's 300% more.
- We have to pay an extra $3,300 per man, woman, and child of "hidden taxes" in the price of goods for the cost of added regulations mandated to the private sector.
- 1996 represented the highest inflation-adjusted taxes ($22,000) ever paid in history for a median-income dual-earner family, and new records were set every year after.
- In 1939, 26 years after the 16th Amendment was adopted, only 5% of the population was

required to file tax returns. Today, it's more than 80%.

- 43% of couples are being penalized by tax laws for being married. Average marriage penalty tax is $1,131 per couple.[57]

Say Hello to Another Problem

It is important to understand that just as taxes will increase in the future, so will the cost of living. Between taxes and the cost of living, there is very little room to increase personal savings for the future. Yet everyone is telling you that you will have to save more. Still, every effort to save is confronted by increasing taxation and increased risks. This creates an enormous amount of debt.

- The cost of education continues to increase.
- The cost of health care and insurance rise every day.
- Property taxes are higher even as property values fall.
- The cost of heat, energy, and gas has gone through the roof.
- Property-insurance premiums have increased rapidly.
- Food costs are higher.
- Average household credit-card debt soars.

---

[57] http://mwhodges.home.att.net/.

- Federal tax increased 2.5 times faster than the economy.[58]
- Automobile, clothing, and daily essentials have increased.
- Personal savings are the lowest since 1934.
- Government social spending has grown 10 times faster than the economy.[59]

The Next Reality Show: Your Future

To survive financially in the future, you must be aware of new lessons and have the ability to apply that knowledge in your everyday financial lives. The lessons that are being ignored and are not being taught by traditional planners are the following:

1. The Demographic Impact
2. The Use of Leverage
3. Controlling the Asset
4. Debt as a Financial Tool
5. Lost Opportunity Costs
6. Liquidity, Use, and Control of Your Money

Since these lessons are not being taught, traditional financial planning may cause transfers of

---

[58] http://www.ncpa.org/pi/taxes/pdtx36.html.
[59] http://mwhodges.home.att.net.

your wealth away from you, unknowingly and unnecessarily, thus creating unintended consequences. It is time to enlist a new thought process. Common sense alone will tell you that change is on the way. Knowing of and preparing for these events will give you an opportunity to make better decisions.

The first part of this book introduced you to the Demographic Impact. In the next 3,000 days, we know that events are going to happen due to the changing demographics. These events, if not prepared for, will have a sudden impact on your future.

Lessons

for

Controlling

Wealth

The Silent Lessons of Creating and Controlling Wealth

All too often, we approach a solution to a problem without understanding the total scope of the problem. Einstein once said: It is difficult to solve a problem by using the same thought process that created the problem. Today, we are mired in the same financial lessons that have been etched in stone for more than 50 years. Some of the most dramatic lessons of accumulating and building wealth are contrary to what we hear from the news media, planners, bankers, and other self-proclaimed experts. Real lasting wealth is achieved by understanding the six lessons that basic financial planning has ignored.

These lessons are a far cry from the everyday "put as much as you can into your 401(k) and pay your house off early" plans that are popularized by those who profit the most from them. Their profits will continue until you learn to apply the six principles into your daily lives.

More time and energy are spent on teaching people how to <u>spend</u> money rather than how to <u>save</u> it. People end up unknowingly and unnecessarily giving away most of their wealth and wealth opportunities. I call this phenomenon "Institutionalizing Education Standards." You are taught how to go to the bank and how to rely on government-sponsored programs with blind faith that their programs will serve you well.

Lesson 1: The Demographic Impact

It is clear that there are changes on the way due to the changing demographics. The result of these changes will impact your ability to save money and to maintain the lifestyle that you are accustomed to. These problems could also create more personal debt. A struggle to pay ever-increasing taxes and keep pace with inflation will be a challenge. The government has created many of these problems. They have a simple solution: Cut benefits and raise taxes. Each of these solutions will impact you. Every attempt you make to save money will be confronted with taxes and risk. It is probably safe to say that, in the future for the average American, 50% of retirement income will go towards health care and taxes.

Knowing what is going to happen is part of the solution. If you know taxes are going to go up in the future, why would you want to expose all of your money to future taxation? Yet, from a traditional-thinking standpoint, that's exactly what we are doing. We are maturing into becoming the most perfect taxpayers in the future. Remember, this future offers very little when it comes to tax deductions.

Albert Einstein once said, "Insanity is doing the same thing over and over again and expecting different results." Over the past 50 years, things have changed dramatically and will continue to do so. The problem is, traditional financial thinking hasn't changed much at all (and the band played on). You would think that with all the financial wisdom out there today, that everyone would be better off. The reality is, in the last 20 years, traditional thinking has created a record amount of debt, a record amount of foreclosures, a record number of bankruptcies, a record number of business failures, and a record amount of credit expansion. These events are not predictions or fiction; this is happening now and will continue to happen in the future. The changing demographics will magnify these existing conditions.

Everyone's common goal should be to create as much tax-free wealth as possible in the future. By reading on, you may discover that there are options and opportunities to accomplish this. Some of these solutions could be right in front of you, but you simply were not aware of them.

Lesson 2: Leverage

If an asset is not being used to generate income, then that asset should be used to create wealth. Learning to use leverage as a financial tool should be your goal. You should want to spend the least amount of money to create the most amount of wealth. As an example, Donald Trump would NOT pay $20 million dollars in cash to purchase an office building. He would gather his advisors to discuss how to pay the least amount of money he could to get control of that asset. Then he would work to improve the property, so he could sell it for, let's say, a $5 million dollar profit. If Mr. Trump had paid the whole $20 million dollars in cash and made $5 million dollars by selling it, you could say he received a 25% return on his investment. But by using leverage, what Mr. Trump actually did was to secure the asset by leveraging $2 million dollars to gain control of the asset and then sold it for a $5 million dollar profit. That results in a gain of 250% for Mr. Trump, compared to a gain of 25% if he had simply paid cash for the building.

This is completely different from what the average person is told to do. We are told by professionals to pay off our houses as fast as we can and to forego the use of leverage as a financial tool. Let's face it, if I want to live in a beautiful home, do I want to make the highest monthly payment I can, or the lowest payment I can to live in the same home?

Just as Donald Trump would never pay cash for a piece of property, neither should you. If you buy a $200,000 home with cash and its value goes up $4,000 in the first year, you made a 2% return on that money. If you had made 12 $1,000 payments, the property still went up $4,000; that is a 33%

return on the money you have invested, and that does not take into consideration the tax deductions. One will argue that you will eventually pay more for the property by taking out a longer mortgage, but the reality is that the average person lives in the same home for about eight years. By using leverage, you are trying to maximize your return while using the least amount of money to do it.

Lesson 3: Controlling the Asset

Owning a home, qualified plans, and investments will all be affected by the demographic shifts. Learning to control your assets will be a valuable tool for you as you prepare for the future.

Investing is not about where your money is invested; it's about how you can use money to create wealth. Controlling an asset simply means this: What power do you have to make an asset you own grow in value? Well, you could make improvements to your home; that would increase your home's value. Wouldn't it be nice if you had the same power to increase the value in your 401(k) or retirement accounts? The problem is that you have absolutely no control over increasing the earnings of your 401(k) or retirement portfolio. If you owned a business, you could work harder to try to make your business more profitable. This is different than investing in companies you don't own and hope that these businesses deliver profits for you. If you have the ability to invest in something and drive the value of that investment upwards, then you should do it. Simply guessing that an investment will do well almost reminds me of trying to pick a winning slot machine at a casino.

Involving yourself in stocks and mutual funds will not effectively create ownership and control. You can control the buying or selling of these investments, but the reality is that there is nothing you can do, or power that you have, to increase the value of these investments. In these types of investments, you also have very little control over market fluctuations and future taxes.

Now don't get me wrong: I believe that some investing is necessary, but it is not the only solution. I just do not believe a 401(k) or an IRA is an asset that you control. In those programs, the government sets all the rules and can even change the rules while the game is being played. If you don't play the game by the rules, you will be fined or penalized. All of this under the presumption that you will save on taxes by using these qualified programs. This idea that you will save on taxes may not necessarily be true. You also may have a limited number of investment products that are available to you in the plan. Don't forget that unless you have a Roth Retirement Account, 100% of all the money you put into a 401(k) or traditional IRA will be taxed from dollar one when you take it out. Who knows what the tax rates will be 20 years from now when you start taking your distributions from these plans. If necessary, go back and review our previous discussion about qualified plans. Also, remember, the government has the right to change all the rules for these plans. The government is in control of these plans—not you.

Controlling an asset doesn't mean that the asset has to be totally paid for, but simply leveraged properly. If I want to drive a really nice car, should I pay cash for it (the most I can), only to have it depreciate over a period of time, or should I pay the least amount per month I can to drive the same car? There is no control in making the price of the car go up in the future. The only hope is to limit the losses that I know are going to occur. The choice of paying cash for something or paying in much smaller increments gives me a little more control of my money today.

Lesson 4: Debt as a Financial Tool

Learning to use leverage to control an asset will force you to learn another financial lesson: Learning to use debt as a financial tool is very important yet often misunderstood. There is a difference between good debt and bad debt. Even the banks, when determining whether you qualify for a loan, will put you in one of two categories. To them, you're either a creditor or a debtor. A creditor has the means to pay off a loan at any time he or she wants. A debtor has every good intention of paying off a loan with monthly installments. The banks will measure the amount of risk that they want to take in order to profit from the loan, but in their eyes, they will always favor the creditor.

There is a lot of misinformation on what debt really is. There is good debt and bad debt, and there is also leveraged and unleveraged debt. Leveraged debt is like a mortgage on your house, where you gain control of the asset in return for monthly payments. The value of the house, in this case, offsets the debt owed on the mortgage. Unleveraged debt is like the $10,000 you ran up on your credit card at the casino. There is not an asset or purchase of an asset to offset this debt.

As an example, if you had $40,000 saved in the bank on Monday and, on Tuesday, withdrew the $40,000 to use as the down payment on a $200,000 home, would you now be in debt to the tune of $160,000? It may feel like you are, but the answer is no, not really. You now hold title to an asset worth $200,000. At any time, you can sell off your asset, the home, and pay off the debt. This is only true, of course, if housing prices remain level.

Lesson 5: Liquidity, Use, and Control of Your Money

Two of the lessons one must master to survive in a changing economic climate are: 1) liquidity, use, and control of your money; and,

2) lost opportunity costs that are associated with everything you do with your money.

Knock, Knock

When a financial opportunity comes along, are you in a financial position to take advantage of it? If you had liquidity, use, and control of your money, you might take advantage of an opportunity that comes along if you choose to. But all too often, when real opportunity knocks at the door, no one is prepared to take advantage of it. Let's face it: Opportunity rarely knocks twice. Many average Americans have all of their money tied up in qualified retirement plans and/or tied up in their homes (home equity). Not that those things are bad, but you also must understand the realities of being in that "tied up" position. If opportunity comes knocking, it may be difficult and expensive to get the money from your qualified plans, and, if you're not prepared, it could be a very slow process to get money from the equity in your home.

Lessons 6: Lost Opportunity Costs

A simple definition of lost opportunity cost is this: If you spend a dollar, not only do you lose that dollar, but you also lose the ability to earn money from that dollar for the rest of your life. If you paid

$20,000 cash for a car today, that $20,000 at a 7.2% rate of return in 10 years would have grown to $40,000. So, the lost opportunity cost of paying cash for that car in this example is the additional $20,000 you could have earned. The question is, was there a cheaper way of buying that car while reducing some of your lost opportunity costs?

There Is a Future Cost to Everything

As you can see, these six lessons offer a different path of thinking. These lessons should be the center point of preparing for the coming uncertain financial future. Simply buying the right blend of investments won't solve the problems that you will be facing in the future. You must learn to work your money, so your money will work for you.

The Family Legacy

The Family Legacy

Your share of the government debt is $145,000, and this debt continues to grow every day. Every man, woman, and child owes this amount just to cover all the promises the U.S. Government has made to creditors, retirees, veterans, and the poor.[60]

That $145,000 you owe does not include your personal debt, such as mortgages, credit cards, car loans, college loans, etc. This also doesn't include the impact of increasing income taxes and property taxes. Also not included are the escalating costs of living that seem to increase daily. All of these increases have grown faster than our incomes.

Government officials' and financial professionals' solution to the growing national debt dilemma is simple: You need to save more! How??? Indebtedness is swallowing America, and according to the Bureau of Economic Analysis, saving as a percentage of disposable personal income is at its lowest rate since 1930—during the Great Depression.[61]

Many believe they can make up ground via the stock market. That hope disappears on a daily basis. Some people hope for inheritances, a windfall when their parents pass away. A very small number

---

[60] "Grandfather Economic Report," by Michael Hodges, http://mwhodges.home.att.net.
[61] http://www.bea.gov.

of families leave large estates. According to the Federal Reserve, of the 17% of the population who received inheritances in the early 2000s, the average amount was $48,000.[62]

It should be a surprise to no one that government agencies are projecting significant increases in future taxation. The idea of deferring taxes to a later date and a higher rate is not a good idea.

Currently, the near future crisis is a four-headed monster that no one is attempting to slay. Right now, American Consumers are:

- Devoid of personal savings,
- In credit card debt up to their eyeballs,
- Working in a historic time where salaries are not keeping up with inflation, and
- Mortgaged to the hilt on houses that are grossly overvalued.

David Walker, the former Comptroller General of the United States, was quoted in an AP interview: "I believe the country faces a critical crossroad and that the decisions that are made—or not made—within the next 10 years or so will have a profound effect on the future of our country, our children, and our grandchildren. The problem gets bigger every day, and the tidal wave gets closer every day."[63]

The big question is, what can you do to put yourself in a better financial situation?

---

[62] Peterson, Peter G. *Running on Empty*. Picador. New York, 2004.
[63] "AP Poll, Analysis, Sound Alarm on National Debt," by Robert Tanner, Associated Press, August 28, 2005.

You Can't Be Aware of Something You're Not Aware Of

Imagine all of the opportunities in life that you missed or that passed you by simply because you were not aware of them. I would like to discuss with you an opportunity that you may have that you're not aware of because no one has taken the time to discuss it with you. I believe that this opportunity could be so critical to your financial future that you should be made aware of the information, even if it is to say "no" to the opportunity. How can you say yes or no to ideas you don't even know exist? All too often, we are not exposed to situations that could really change our lives.

For years, planning professionals have operated under the theory that reducing retirement income and reducing the size of an estate is the best way to reduce the taxation that one must face. The real concern should be centered on how to leave the most money and create the most wealth for your family or your favorite charities. If planning doesn't do this, what good is it? The goal should be to maximize your wealth with the least amount of money, and eliminate costs and taxes while securing the future for your heirs.

Can You Spare Some Change?

It is my observation that, for the past 50 years, the foundation of the financial services industry hasn't changed very much. I believe marketing and the media have made us more aware of financial products and services, and technology has made it easier to get involved, but the solutions have remained the same.

The average person is really limited in the options he or she can pursue financially. Traditional thinking can be broken down very easily. You can invest in the stock market; you can invest in real estate; you can invest in bank savings vehicles; and you can invest in retirement plans. The one thing that remains constant with these planning options is that you, the consumer, are the only one at risk in these ventures.

Mr. Hyde, I Presume?

These types of investments come complete with dual personalities. Not only can you earn a few dollars, but they can also create a number of transfers of your wealth in the future. Traditional thinking could expose you to possible losses in the market. You could be charged fees for accounts, managers, and for maintenance, regardless of whether your accounts earn money or not. You may also have to pay income tax and capital gains tax, and there may be estate tax implications that you will face in the future. To summarize, over the past 50 years, very little has changed in the traditional approach to planning and its consequences.

<u>Poverty Planning</u>:
It Takes No Time
It Takes No Effort
Results Are Guaranteed

All too often, I see people doing the very basics, financially. With their heads buried in the sand, they take the ostrich approach to planning. Their "wait and see" retirement strategy suits them well. Then, with limited or no financial knowledge, they attempt to survive in a world created for them by the government. They have been told that their pension and retirement savings will be enough to live on in their golden years. Let us not forget Social Security. But, the ever-increasing cost of living, increasing taxation, and increasing cost of insurance drain the foundation of their future planning away. Often, they end up looking for part-time jobs after retirement. Pride, fear, and laziness fuel the ignorance of poverty planning. They receive financial advice from their friends and neighbors, but remain skeptical of anyone with professional knowledge. They work and work and never get ahead, and leave very little behind when they die. Unfortunately, they pass on the same financial lessons to their children as a legacy.

The Defining Moment

I have had the opportunity on a few occasions to speak at the Federal Reserve of Chicago's Money Smart Week. To my surprise, a segment of my speech received the highest reviews and was subsequently aired on local television stations. I was humbled by the praise I received, but more important than that was the message that was delivered and the public's response to it. Remember, you can't be aware of something that you're not aware of. With that thought in mind, I would like to share with you a thought and an idea that could change your life forever.

The Vanishing Legacy

With the final breath, it all ended. All the lifelong dreams, the fifty years of work, raising a family, the pain of losses, the memory of joys and happiness: gone. Now, all that is left of that life are the memories of that person and the legacy of a lifetime. To those left behind, the memories are theirs to keep, but everything else must be divided into two categories: what they are allowed to keep and what the government claims to be theirs. What is truly unfortunate is that the government claims must be settled first and what is left is divided between creditors of the deceased and members of the family.

A hundred years ago, it was not uncommon for farms to be worked and owned by a family. The grandparents were there working and contributing to the farm, along with their middle-aged children and their grandchildren. The family structure was whole. Family pride was evident, and this was passed on generationally. The older members of the family were well aware of the idea of legacy. They worked hard to create a better life for the next generation. The farm, along with the memories, was their legacy.

Today, that element of a family legacy has almost disappeared. Although there are loving memories, the passing of the family "farm," today known as family wealth, has been mismanaged into nonexistence. Interference from the government and an enormous lack of financial knowledge, along with pride and ignorance, rob families from passing tremendous amounts of wealth to the next generation. Along with it goes the lasting family legacy.

When no one pays attention to the everyday details of the farm, it will no longer be a productive entity to pass on, and, in many cases, it will become a burden and a debt to the next generation of the family. Today, the idea of viewing the family as a single unit has been ignored by almost everyone, yet it remains as one of the only solutions for creating lasting family wealth, generationally. The passing of the family wealth (the farm) doesn't occur accidentally. It is planned and well thought out. Rich people do this often, and their families remain rich. Poorer families, although their lives may prosper, believe in taking it with them when they die. Their legacy is usually a home, some savings, and other (for lack of a better word) stuff. Although those things have value, they lack in comparison to what could have been passed on had the entire family planned the family legacy seriously.

The idea of keeping wealth in the family is opposed vigorously by the government because they have a harder time getting their hands on this money via taxes. Many politicians try to pit the rich against the middle class; all the while, the middle class aspires to be rich, pursuing their financial dreams via the Lotto and casinos. The difference comes down to this: Some families guarantee their ongoing legacy, while others gamble it away.

The Social Fiber of the Country

The United States started to lose an important social foundation in the 1960s. Crisis after crisis, from Vietnam to civil rights, the drug culture to presidential assassinations, the once starry-eyed nation woke up with a reality hangover that would plague it forever. What would suffer the most in this historic time would be the family structure. The "What's in it for me" and the "I want it now" generation blossomed and grew up to train and educate the next generation, flaunting the wisdom of ME and I.

The family social structure, once the cornerstone of ethics and morality, started to crumble, and with it, family opportunities also crumbled. The growth of single-parent families left little room for financial success. Government social engineering only created more problems and greater dependence for its so-called "free" benefits. That dependency aided the problem, not the solution. The aftereffects of the loss of the family structure continue to cost the government billions of dollars. Along with the costs are increasing crime rates, suicide rates, divorce rates, abortion rates, personal debt, and bankruptcy rates. All of these have a direct correlation to the loss of the family structure.

Institutionalizing Educational Standards

With the fall of the family structure, the liberalizing of education took on the role of psychologist in making kids feel okay and being sensitive to their every need. The new educational goal is that no one would fail in school. They would only fail after they were out of school. The ability to apply school knowledge to everyday circumstances is nonexistent. Not only is the knowledge missing to grow wealth, but also missing is the family and its ability to grow wealth generationally. In the old days, this would be the equivalent to the grandparents leaving the farm before they taught their kids the farming process. Obviously, nothing would grow, which is why, in today's family, nothing is growing either. More time and energy are spent on teaching you how to <u>spend</u> your money, rather than how to save it. You end up unknowingly and unnecessarily giving away your wealth and wealth opportunities.

If tomorrow you discovered an opportunity that, by planning together with your parents or your kids, could create millions of dollars for your family (or charities), would you take advantage of that opportunity? If you also discovered that the money could be transferred to your family, guaranteed and tax-free, would you do it? I have reasons to believe that you were not taught how to do this in school, <u>any</u> school.

Creating the Legacy

It came to my attention while visiting the San Diego Zoo that every animal display had something in common. Each one of them was funded or sponsored by a family or family foundation, a/k/a generational family wealth. The question that came to my mind was: What did these families do that others didn't or don't do? The revelation hit me like a ton of bricks: They leverage the least amount of money to create the most amount of wealth by investing in their family. The rich follow three basic rules to accomplish this:

RULE NUMBER ONE: In your family, use the least amount of money to create the greatest amount of wealth.

RULE NUMBER TWO: Guarantee the wealth will occur and that the legacy will transfer tax-free.

RULE NUMBER THREE: Create multiples of wealth immediately.

That was the answer. It was clear, and believe me, it was the best trip to the zoo I ever experienced. On the way home, though, one thought kept echoing through my head: Rich people think like rich people; poor people think like poor people. It was troubling. I asked myself one question: Would someone want to create wealth for his family if he didn't have to spend one more dime than he was spending right now? If you could realign your assets to make wealth possible and still retain control of the money, would you do it? The key to all of this is to consider the family as an investment.

Controlling the Asset

Investing is not about <u>where</u> your money is; it's about how you can <u>use it</u> to create wealth. This is far different from buying a stock and praying that the stock will go up. Warren Buffett never buys 100 shares and just holds it. He, like Mark Cuban, buys shares of a stock to get some level of CONTROL of the company. If you have the resources to take control of a company and you think it's a great investment, do it. If you want to try to guess on some companies, buy their stock, and hope it goes up, then you might as well go to Las Vegas, because you have no advantage at all to CONTROL the value of that stock.

In the old days, the family had total CONTROL of the farm. The family could affect the growth and outcome of the farm they owned and CONTROLLED. Today, in generating family wealth, dabbling in stocks and mutual funds doesn't provide the ownership and control that is needed to pass on wealth successfully. The elements that affect these types of legacies are taxes, risk, creditors, and luck. In defense of many who follow this strategy, professional advice has told them this is the only way to create wealth.

Leverage

Unfortunately, following traditional invest-ment plans does not create multiples of wealth immediately. If a family asset is not being used to generate income, then that asset should be used to create family generational wealth. You would want to insure and guarantee that the wealth be transferred to the family tax-free. Most importantly, you would want to expend the least amount of money to create the most wealth. This is known as *leverage*.

The Contract

If you were able to invest in an older member of your family and they allowed you to do so to create the ultimate family legacy, what investment would be used? Life insurance. It is the perfect solution for family wealth creation. It is a contract the family CONTROLS. The cash values and death benefit grow tax-deferred and tax-free. It is protected from creditors and passes outside of probate. Any number of family members, including the parents, can contribute to the premiums. This creates the greatest amount of family legacy that will pass on to the family, using the least amount of money. All of this is centered on the legacy of love.

This will be a very emotional decision and should be viewed with the proper perspective. In the old days, all members of the family would invest all their time and money to increase the wealth of the farm, knowing someday it would be theirs. They didn't do this out of greed, but out of love for the family.

To Whom It May Concern

I would like to address this issue of the Family Legacy on two different levels: the older crowd (you know who you are) and their children, who are probably 30 years old or older.

Lifelong Dreams

I was speaking to an elderly group of people, and I asked them a very direct question: "How many dreams and goals that you had when you were 20 years old actually came true in your lifetime?" The room was quiet. Many felt fortunate just to be there. They had just seen the wicked turns that life can take and the stings of disappointment. But, they all did have one thing in common: They all wished things could have been a little bit better.

"Everyone here probably got married and started thinking about raising a family. Children were born, and reality set in. It is very expensive to raise kids. Some of the initial dreams you had when you got married had to be set aside. The idea of providing for your kids became first and foremost. You wanted to provide a better life for your children, even at the sacrifice of your dreams.

"Your kids grew up, went to college, and moved on, and you realized you had to start saving for your own retirement. Once again, dreams and goals were set aside to avoid the crisis of not having enough money at retirement. You saved and saved, with what seemed like very little progress, while giving up the things you really wanted in life.

"Retirement comes. You've made it. The lifestyle you have been accustomed to may have had to change somewhat, but you're okay. You have time to reflect back on your lives and wonder: What would have happened if you had been able to fulfill your dreams? Would your entire family have benefited from your success? And would these dreams have created a legacy to give to your family?

"Today, if you had the magic to recapture all the dreams and goals that you had during your lifetime and give them to your children and grandchildren without spending one more dime than you are already spending, would you do it? It is possible that the opportunity is right before you today, but you are simply not aware of it."

Opportunity of My Lifetime

I would like to share with you an example of how the Family Legacy can dramatically impact your life. First of all, you have to make your family aware that this opportunity exists, as I did with my family. I held a family meeting to discuss the situation.

I told my family that I was deeply concerned about the path that we are headed as a country and a society. I told them that I was fearful of the changes that would affect their lives and the impact it would have on their ability to survive financially in the future. I asked them that if they had an opportunity to prepare for this uncertain future without spending one more dime than they were already spending, would they do it? I looked at them and said, "The opportunity to do this is right in front of you sitting at this table."

You see, I wanted to give my family an opportunity of a lifetime. I wanted to create a family legacy that would be the foundation for not only their financial future but also for their children, my grandchildren. I realized that my children now had their own families, and their ability to build real, lasting wealth was limited. I told them that I knew their future would be challenged by fluctuations in the investment markets, and the future tax increases were a certainty due to the tremendous changes in

LEONARD RENIER

the demographics in the near future. In my discussion with them, I wanted them to seek out every opportunity that we had as a family to create real wealth. The goal was to spend the least amount of money to create the most amount of tax-free wealth without any additional money being spent.

I took a second and told them: Rich people think like rich people; poor people think like poor people. The difference between the two is that most rich people insure and guarantee that their wealth will be passed on to their families tax-free. Well, the real truth is that most of us are not rich. I said, "I would also like to pass on as much wealth to you as I possibly can. I would like to use my life to maximize the amount of money that I can offer you." It was quiet at the table, and I said, "The opportunity to accomplish this is sitting right in front of you. I want to offer you the opportunity to invest in me. I want to do this out of love, as a family legacy for you and my grandchildren."

The Legacy Opportunity

The obvious response from everyone, including my family, is: How do we do this? Well, there are really a lot of ways to create a family legacy. People simply are not aware of them. You see, you cannot be aware of something that you're not aware of. An example of one of the ways I could create a legacy for my family could be presented as follows.

Creating the legacy I discussed with my family would not involve one dime of my money, nor would any members of my family spend any more money than they are already spending. This would be their investment in me. We needed a vehicle that gave them tremendous financial rewards, utilized the least amount of their money, and would pass the money to them tax-free. As rich people do, we insured and guaranteed that these things would occur. They purchased a life insurance contract on me with the highest paying death benefit, using the least amount of premium they could to fund it. To pay for this, they stopped over-funding their 401(k)s and outside investments, and stopped making any additional payments to mortgage principal. Between them, this came to a nice sum of money. My kids are in their early thirties. If I lived another 10 years and the death benefit came due (i.e. I died), the internal rate of return on their investment in me would be about 36%, tax-free. If I lived another 20 years instead of 10 years, the internal rate of return would be 13%, tax-free. Even at the age of 80, the internal rate of return would be about 10%, and would create about $1.7 million dollars for them, tax-free, upon my death. My kids would own the policy and have access to the values in it, even while I was alive. It is also possible for me to contribute additional money to this contract to increase the amount of the legacy to my family.

IMPORTANT NOTICE
**The example above is just an example, and the
numbers used are only estimations, and will be
different for everyone. Premiums differ from
company to company. Age, health, and
insurability will affect premiums. To see if you
qualify and to get internal rates of return,
contact an experienced, licensed professional.**

My example was meant to be simplistic in
nature, yet create dramatic results. There are many
ways, in a family setting, to create and fund a
Family Legacy and, at the same time, reduce future
taxation. It also addresses the issues of a financial
future that is filled with uncertainty. This is not a
trendy solution that fades as markets change; rather,
it is a solid foundation for creating wealth in the
future. The legacy increases the family's money
supply now and in the future. It creates more and
better benefits for you and your family. The legacy
reduces the amount of risk and future taxation that
you would typically be exposed to. It is also
possible that all of this can be achieved without
spending one more dime than you're already
spending.

Knowing what is going to happen in the near
future can give you a distinct advantage in
preparing for the challenge ahead. The sudden
impact of the demographic changes will affect

everyone. Higher taxes and one's ability to save are major concerns in the future. Imagine the idea of creating future wealth in a family and having it pass tax-free. Now imagine waking up tomorrow knowing that your future was financially secure. How would your life change? All of this can happen if you understand a few simple lessons: the use of leverage; controlling the asset; debt as a financial tool; liquidity, use, and control of your money; and lost opportunity costs. These lessons will help you reduce the transfers of your wealth that are occurring every day, unknowingly and unnecessarily. Recapturing these transfers could help you create a family legacy.

Rich people think like rich people; poor people think like poor people. Once again, the difference between the two is rich people know how to secure their wealth for the next generation. First, they know how to use the least amount of money to create the most amount of wealth. Second, the rich guarantee that the wealth will occur and that the legacy will transfer tax-free. Finally, they create multiples of wealth in the legacy immediately. This is exactly what I did in my example with my family. I did this for my family to give them at least a fighting chance to survive in a future that has been discussed in this book. Is the family legacy the solution to all the future problems? No, but it's a powerful tool for building a secure future for the ones you love.

Why I Did This

It is my concern that the path we are on financially, both personally and as a country, will have an impact on everyone. This book was meant to make you aware of something that you possibly were not aware of. The challenges we will be forced to confront due to the dramatically changing demographics and the course that has been set by the politicians we elect will financially be overwhelming. Unfortunately, as a society, we may drown in debt. People who now realize the problems that are coming can now focus on solutions and get prepared. The book was also meant to introduce you to ideas and opportunities that will help guide you through this uncertain future. It was also meant to create questions in your mind, so you can have a serious discussion with a professional who has been trained to give you educated answers. Everyone's situation, opportunities, and solutions will be different.

With all the perils that are confronting you in the future, you owe it to yourself and your family to prepare for the Sudden Impact.